Women Working in Nontraditional Fields

references and resources

1963–1988

G. K. Hall

WOMEN'S STUDIES

Publications

Barbara Haber
Editor

Women Working in Nontraditional Fields

references and resources

1963–1988

Carroll Wetzel Wilkinson

G.K. Hall & Co.

Boston, Massachusetts

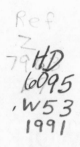

First published 1991
by G.K. Hall & Co.
70 Lincoln Street
Boston, Massachusetts 02111

10 9 8 7 6 5 4 3 2 1

Library of Congress Cataloging-in-Publication Data

Wilkinson, Carroll Wetzel.
    Women working in nontraditional fields : reference and resources,
1963-1988 / Carol Wetzel Wilkinson.
      p. cm.
    Includes indexes.
    ISBN 0-8161-8934-X
    1. Women – Employment – United States – Bibliography. I. Title
Z7963.E7W53 1991
[HD6095]
016.3314 – dc20   90-26655
                                               CIP

The paper used in this publication meets the minimum requirements of
American National Standard for Information Sciences – Permanence of
Paper for Printed Library Materials. ANSI Z39.48-1984.   ∞™
MANUFACTURED IN THE UNITED STATES OF AMERICA

Contents

Preface

The original plan for this book called for a comprehensive compilation of a reference bibliography of twenty-five years of publishing about women at work in all nontraditional fields. I intended to include all information I found about the subject in general, and then I planned to select eighteen specific fields from six basic job classification groups to document. The context from which I approached this work was established in my article "Work: Challengers to Occupational Segregation," published in 1985.[1] The research strategy for this book was based on the assumption (charted in that article) that all work can be divided into six basic classified groups. They are high technology, the arts, the professions, the trades, public life, and a miscellaneous grouping. In the end, I chose in this book to concentrate on trades, professions (including some careers in the arts), technological fields, and an assortment of jobs in areas such as sports, the clergy, law enforcement, and agriculture. Within all of these groups there are particular occupations, jobs, and career choices that are still considered unusual for women, even if the oddity factor is now modified somewhat. The general literature about women in nontraditional fields is listed before the literature about particular jobs.

The landmark books and articles I discovered along the way required more attention and time than I am accustomed to in bibliographical analysis. I could not simply document the literature; I felt I needed to point out to users of the book various relationships between the general and specific materials. Trends were emerging; themes of urgency were begging for identification. I wanted to create a cognitive map of the frontier, a crazy quilt with strong seams, to provide some kind of unity for the many voices speaking in isolation and for the fields whose literature I did get to examine. American society at large and the women who are on the occupational frontier need to grasp the ramifications of their contributions and the agenda that lies ahead if real social progress is going to be achieved.

It soon became apparent that comprehensive coverage of the literature of all fields working women have integrated would not be possible in one book. The volume of the vast and flourishing literature uncovered during my research prevented it. The volume of publishing in this area during the late 1970s and early to mid-1980s increased dramatically. This paralleled women's social advancements and the concurrent progress in women's studies research. My progress slowed as the volume of publications increased. Goal reassessment became essential if I was to meet even an extended publication deadline.

This great increase in resources clearly indicated a need for a new structure for the presentation of materials. The modified strategy for this book's creation became instead compilation of a sourcebook of qualitative, bibliographic analysis of a significant portion of the twenty-five years of literature on women in nontraditional occupations. The structure for presentation changed to general materials followed by specific ones. Of necessity, the scope of this book also had to be limited to those sources which I could acquire and analyze. When I have included entries without annotations, this simply means that I was unable to analyze a copy of the material in time for publication but felt it was important enough to include in the hope that others' research would be advanced. The book still makes accessible a significant literature of women in nontraditional fields in general, as well as subliteratures of many specific fields, though not as many as originally intended. Most often, the women in specific fields I chose to include made up only 1-5 percent of the total work force, never the 25 percent the basic working definition of nontraditional jobs called for. Thus the references to the jobs of astronaut, pilot, rabbi, jockey, farmer, and fire fighter.

Another reason for the altered strategy was that I wanted to be able to include references to works that examine the full diversity of women's work experience in nontraditional fields, including issues of race, sex, class, and ethnic differences. The literature focusing on these subjects is less accessible, being scattered in special collections around the country. Time and travel limitations have impeded full success in this area, but I have made a beginning by traveling to and working in collections whose goals are to collect literature on behalf of all women. My coverage of this area is thus by no means exhaustive; it is rather meant to be a sampling and a starting point for further research.

I have consciously chosen to include nonacademic, small-press, and government publications to make a more democratic assessment and representation of thought. I did not want to include work done exclusively in the academy; I wanted to balance that important work with the thoughts of independent feminists writing in publications with small circulations and of women who are actually working in nontraditional workplaces. These writings examine trends and issues for women who have challenged occupational segregation, vocational and career education and counseling for women, lifetime career options for women in nontraditional fields, and implications for employers managing a sexually integrated workplace where women represent a tiny minority. The subject has required these perspectives in order to maintain its integrity.

Preparation for this project included thorough examination of relevant bibliographies, indexes, and reference sources as well as reading and analysis of the literature of the subject that emerged during the initial research. I also made trips to explore and use the special resources of several important collections on women and work. Highly relevant materials were located at the Marguerite Rawalt Resource Center in Washington, D.C., and the Arthur and Elizabeth Schlesinger Library on the History of Women in America at Radcliffe College in Cambridge, Massachusetts. Further help of great value came through explorations of the materials at the Midwest Women's Center in Chicago, Illinois, where training is given to women entering nontraditional fields, and the resources of the Midwest branch of the Women's Bureau of the U.S. Department of Labor, also in Chicago.

Overall, this book is divided into sections that make the vast literature under study more manageable. Users will find general materials about women working in a variety of nontraditional, male-intensive jobs in one section. Materials specific to individual jobs are placed in appropriately titled subsections of their own. Materials on related and intersecting issues of importance that emerged during the study also have sections of their own. These publications include explorations of the dynamics of tokenism, of career and job choice, and of the changing workplaces where employers are beginning to see the economic necessity of rooting out environmental harassment.

These sections are only the first level of organization, however. The index of subjects provides access to a deeper level of analysis and users should refer to it for entries scattered throughout the text that are related. Many subliteratures can be uncovered in this manner. Title and author indexes are also provided to aid in locating the work of particular individuals or definite opening keywords.

This bibliography and sourcebook contains 737 citations to primarily printed information published between 1963 and 1988. Each entry is numbered. These numbers are used in the author, title, and subject indexes for ease of access to references. Of these, over 590 are annotated. The book includes references to journal and popular magazine articles, books and book chapters, dissertations, government publications, and an assortment of handbooks, directories, research reports, pamphlets, training manuals, and career promotion booklets all relating to fields of work still thought unusual for women in our society.

Notes

1. Carroll Wetzel Wilkinson, "Work: Challenges to Occupational Segregation," in *The Women's Annual,* no. 5, ed. Mary Drake McFeely (Boston: G.K. Hall & Co., 1985), 149-67.

Acknowledgments

Solitude and connectedness have been intertwined inextricably throughout the four years it has taken to create this book. Through my support networks at home, at the WVU libraries, in my West Virginia community, and around the country, special people have given me a hospitable environment in which to work and a safe place to retreat when the work of the day was done. To do the research, analysis, and writing I was alone, but it was a thoroughly supported and respected isolation. This gift is one I deeply value and wish to acknowledge.

My colleagues in the West Virginia University Faculty Senate supported eight weeks of research leave in 1987; the West Virginia University Office of Academic Affairs supported six weeks of leave during the summer of 1988 and four weeks of leave during the summer of 1989. Those five months over a three-year period were crucial in developing the focus and concentration I needed to complete this book. I wish to thank warmly William Reeves of the Office of Sponsored Programs at WVU; Dr. Frank Franz, the provost of West Virginia University; Paula Jones, the special assistant to the provost; and the WVU dean of libraries, Dr. Ruth M. Jackson. Their personal and institutional support has been invaluable as I completed this project; it has also expanded the boundaries and expectations for academic librarians in the research environment of West Virginia University.

Further financial support for substantial research expenses including travel, manuscript preparation, and computer consultations was provided by the West Virginia Humanities Foundation, the West Virginia Alliance for Women's Studies, and the West Virginia University Regional Research Institute. I warmly thank Bob Weiss, Mildred Bright, Dr. Judith Stitzel, and

Dr. Andrew Isserman for their encouragement and financial investment in the promise and significance of this research.

That said, I wish to go further in my acknowledgment of Judith Stitzel's contribution to this project. From the beginning, she saw the validity of and need for the reference book I was creating. Long before the WVU libraries were able to support the research, she, through the resources at the Center for Women's Studies, provided a base of operations and a core of personal, financial, and intellectual sustenance.

She has also been a constant and productive source of inspiration for the courage it takes to find additional financial support. I needed this help and it was given generously through the four years of the project. I thank her for all of these dedicated and meaningful contributions as a friend, agent, and mentor. Her late assistant, Judith Mossberg, also gave time and nourishment to the project by arranging travel plans, providing ready encouragement, and thinking of alternative sources of money when the last source had refused support. I want to acknowledge how much her contributions meant to me and how much I miss her.

Critical technical support in manuscript preparation was provided throughout the three years of creation and revision by my trusted friend Rose M. Bell. I wish gratefully to acknowledge both her remarkable skill and her enduring patience. Keith Walton patiently assisted every step of the way with endless hardware and software consultations and expert technical advice and support. Kathleen Speaker excelled as the author and title indexer of this challenging volume. Kelly Pasco assisted ably during the final stages of first-draft technical production. Their contributions have strengthened both the quality of the book and my mental health. I could not have done this without them.

The collections and people at several libraries have made important contributions to this book as well. Much of the research for this book was done in the libraries of West Virginia University, but there were times when we did not have the sources I needed. I wish to thank my colleague Penny Pugh and her assistant Judi McCracken for their tenacious pursuit of materials on my behalf through the effective national interlibrary loan system.

The staff at the Schlesinger Library for the History of Women in America, the Marguerite Rawalt Resource Center at the Business and Professional Women's Foundation in Washington, D.C., and the Midwest Women's Center Library in Chicago were all wonderful to me, and I offer special thanks to Barbara Haber at the Schlesinger Library and Michelle Schroll at the Rawalt Center for their enthusiastic and respectful encouragement. Barbara Haber served also as an advisory reader during the late stages of revision and her comments strengthened the presentation of material significantly.

My mother-in-law, Jule Porter Wilkinson, herself an editor of many books, provided a loving summer home where I could work independently on my vacations, and she relentlessly supported me from afar knowing as no one else could what I really needed to get the work done. I warmly acknowledge the way she strengthened me with her precious assistance.

My husband, Christopher Wilkinson, has been a frier d, guide, and partner through the whole creation process. His loving encouragement and his persistent confidence in me have been the central components of the connectedness I have described here. With his enthusiastic support, I am more effective and vital. He has inspired me in both private and public spheres and I want to acknowledge these beautiful gifts.

Samuel Wilkinson, our ten-year-old son, has lovingly endured the solitude I have needed for the project while also contributing great ideas for fun when the work was over. I thank him for his generosity, patience, and love.

All the members of the staff in the Circulation Department at the Wise Library have fostered my research with effective delivery of departmental services and research support, and I thank each of them for faithfully standing by me over the four years of the project. Selected members of library faculty in the Reference Department have also generously supported this work. I especially wish to thank Kathleen Key.

I thank the members of G.K. Hall's editorial and production staff who worked diligently with me on this book. They include Michael Sims, India Koopman, Ara Salibian, John Amburg, and Henriette Campagne. Elizabeth Holthaus, executive editor of the reference program, led us all through the process, and I extend warm thanks to her for her fortitude and good humor.

Finally, I take full responsibility for any omissions and errors in the text of this book. I want to close by thanking the many thousands of women in the United States who work in fields where there are large numbers of men and very few women. During the last decade, I have been interested in what they were going through personally and in the meaning of their work in relation to our society. Labor or management, white- or blue-collar, women's presence in male-intensive fields of work makes a critical contribution to workplace redefinition. In the decade ahead, perhaps more nontraditional workplaces will become welcoming and satisfying for women as they develop their careers side by side with men. Women in male-intensive fields of work are on a real frontier, which, like all frontiers, presents difficult challenges and hardships. In time, I hope their self-acceptance, awareness of full personhood, and workplace environments all improve.

Introduction to a
Literature of Integrated Outsiders

In 1961 President John F. Kennedy charged the country's first Commission on the Status of Women to explore partnerships between men and women in all aspects of American life. He wanted to "eliminate all barriers to the full partnership of women in our democracy."[1] One wonders, looking back thirty years, what the president thought full partnership between men and women meant. Admirable steps were taken at the time to remove barriers for women's access to jobs, and slowly this country has seen small numbers of women enter fields that were once thought to be exclusively male domains. But real partnership in work does not come easily even in the 1990s.

Was the president thinking of the sort of partnership that Fred Astaire and Ginger Rogers had on the dance floor and to which Ann Richards referred in her keynote address to the Democratic National Convention in 1988? "If you give us a chance, we can perform," she said. "After all, Ginger Rogers did everything Fred Astaire did. She just did it backwards and in high heels."[2] Such double standards have been insidious and pervasive in our society. President Kennedy was no doubt thinking of the development of full human potential when he raised the idea of partnership and inaugurated the agenda for the Commission on the Status of Women. But he probably did not have a full grasp of the contortions a woman has to go through (on and off the dance floor) while developing her potential capacities, especially if she wishes to work side by side with men in a field where men have predominated for generations.

Kennedy established the commission to combat "prejudices and outmoded customs which act as barriers to the full realization of women's basic rights which should be fostered as part of our nation's commitment to human dignity, freedom, and democracy."[3]

Largely through the efforts of Ethel Peterson, Woman's Bureau director and assistant secretary of labor under Kennedy, equal employment opportunity for women began its development as a national policy during the 1960s.[4] The commission investigated women's position in American society and drew up an agenda of desirable reforms to find ways to encourage women to make their full contributions as citizens.

In the area of employment, the commission concluded that the most feasible tool for directing employers' attention to the importance of equal treatment for women workers in hiring, training, and promotion was an executive order mandating new governing principles in private employment.[5] Executive Order 10980 required the commission to "review progress and make recommendations as needed for constructive action in employment policies and practices, federal and state labor laws, and additional affirmative steps which should be taken through legislation, executive or administrative action to ensure nondiscrimination on the basis of sex and to enhance constructive employment opportunities for women."

The commission recommended other reforms, including expansion of part-time employment opportunities; discontinuation of "men only" and "women only" jobs in the civil service; altering negative attitudes toward women's absenteeism and quit rates; equalization of rates of advancement between men and women; and challenging outdated beliefs about women as supervisors. The commission gathered the first firm data on many phases of women's employment and placed the facts in the hands of the personnel policy makers of the nation's largest employer.[6]

In her comments on the work of the commission, Margaret Mead stated that the report "is a review of progress that has been made in giving American women practical equality with men educationally, economically, and politically." She further pointed out that "stated very simply, it is at present assumed that any barrier whatsoever to full participation on the level of the privileged, white, adult, American male should be treated as a handicap so that it can be overcome. All should have the chances to win the prizes offered in life's race."[7] The "progress toward practical equality" that Margaret Mead spoke of in 1965 is further charted in this book. Practical equality is not yet enjoyed by all women in nontraditional fields.

In 1990 partnership brings to mind full equality of rights, autonomy, sharing, and personhood. It is not the opportunity to dance backwards in high heels. Kennedy's idea of partnership was surely not the same in depth of understanding about expectations of partnership as ours is today. We imagine equal numbers of women and men side by side in positions of power, influence, and authority in every kind of career in the work force, without any trace of oppression or discrimination. Thirty years ago, Kennedy was thinking about the opportunity to be a partner. We think now about the harrowing process of becoming a partner and the small numbers of women who are true partners with men in work, education, and politics. This book provides access to a variety of materials that document the far-reaching, complex changes that have taken place for women in nontraditional fields since Kennedy's commission filed its report.

Historical Background

Before the 1960s American women worked in unusual jobs, of course. Women have always worked in the United States, whether or not society accepted the type of work they chose and whether or not they were paid for their labors. These facts are well established by the new scholarship in many fields, most notably history and sociology. Issues of the history of women at work have been explored scrupulously in recent years by feminist scholars including Alice Kessler-Harris and Anne Firor Scott.

There is evidence of a few individual women here and there since the 1600s doing what society proclaimed as men's work in many fields. For example, Dinah Nuthead of Annapolis, Maryland, received a license to run her husband's printing business after his death in 1696.[8] And Frances Baker of Detroit, Michigan, worked as a deep-water diver in 1905 helping to locate and rescue ships that had sunk in the Great Lakes.[9] No doubt there are hundreds of undocumented women who, since colonial settlement, have earned their livings in this country by doing work that, according to social custom, belonged to men.

It is also well known that there are precedents for integration of groups of women into previously all-male fields. The best known precedent occurred during the Second World War in technical fields as part of the government-sponsored war effort to integrate women into industrial production of ships and other needed equipment. Unfortunately, the women lost their jobs as soon as the war ended and men could return to "their" jobs.

Beginning in 1963 with the Equal Pay Act amendment to the Fair Labor Standards Act, which made classifications such as "men's jobs" and "women's jobs" illegal, there has been significant legislative progress toward the goal of eliminating sex discrimination in employment in the United States. Subsequent breakthroughs include Title VII of the Civil Rights Act of 1964 as amended by the Equal Employment Opportunity Act of 1972, the Pregnancy Discrimination Act of 1978, and Executive Order 11246 as amended by Executive Order 11375.

All of these legislative initiatives bar hiring based on stereotyped characterizations of the sexes, classification or labeling of "men's jobs" and "women's jobs," and advertising under "male" or "female" headings. The executive orders required federal contracts to include language by which contractors pledge not to discriminate against any employee or applicant for employment because of sex, race, color, religion, age, or national origin. The contractor must further pledge to take affirmative action to ensure nondiscriminatory treatment. Such action must include employment, upgrading, demotion, or transfer; recruitment or recruitment advertising; layoff or other forms of compensation; and selection for training, including apprenticeships.

Although documentation does exist of a few extraordinary women who worked in highly unusual jobs in the United States from 1696 on, it only proves that there were exceptions to the rule of sexual segregation at work. Until the aforementioned legislation's effects began to take hold in the 1970s, it was not possible for larger numbers of women in America to integrate higher paying, more prestigious fields with hope of having even a few female coworkers.

In the early 1970s, noticeable numbers of women began to get jobs in unusual fields and stay in them. This happened in growing numbers of work areas that had previously been closed. New terminology began appearing in the popular press referring to "nontraditional jobs," defined as "those predominantly held by men and considered atypical for women, such as managers, machinists, and craftworkers."[10] Photographs accompanied newspaper articles headlined "Women in Nontraditional Fields" in the *New York Times,* for example, in 1972.[11] No one is sure where the terminology came from.

As previously mentioned, part of the reason for this change was legal. Thanks to the legislative developments of the 1960s, by the early 1970s it was no longer legal to maintain exclusively male workplaces. The old barriers against women in, for example, coal mining, horse racing, the ministry, fire fighting, space exploration, and certain medical specializations like surgery began to crack and fall. Women challenged the old barriers and claimed their right to do the work of their choice and to earn salaries equal to men's.

Under normal social conditions, not exceptional war efforts, women were starting to earn their livings by doing "men's work" again and the idea of a male bastion was beginning to seem anachronistic. When analysts could finally examine the census data for 1980 in detail in 1984, they established that there were few, if any, work fields left that women had not integrated.[12]

The changes we see today in the gender proportions in previously all-male fields signal a process of permanent social and psychological change in the United States. The consequences in the workplace demonstrate that some gender barriers have finally been challenged and broken. The popular media now reflect images of women at work in occupations only recently made accessible, such as those of astronaut and carpenter. The developments have also come to the attention of a variety of academic disciplines as the history of this transformation of the work force is charted.

Since the great civil-rights legislation of the 1960s, while racial integration has been becoming a reality, another transformation has been slowly taking place in American society. It is a transformation from a gender-segregated society to a gender-coordinated society.[13] In new ways, particularly from the mid-1970s to the present, men and women have been figuring out new ways to work side by side as equals in both public and private settings. Sexual integration and coordination has come slowly to the American workplace.

In 1989, the newly published and influential *Women's Thesaurus* suggests that the term "nontraditional" should be dropped and the phrase "male-intensive" be used instead. Whatever they are called, there are jobs in American society that are still considered unusual and sometimes exceptional for women to hold. The women in them live with a kind of "fishbowl dynamic" caused by their high visibility. This fact colors their working experience greatly and influences their own perceptions of themselves. The dynamics of tokenism are also evident in the experiences of such women. After all the social progress for women, there is still an underlying sense in certain quarters that women do not belong there.

The reference and research tool I now present to practitioners and scholars is a first look at a literature that bears further study in the future. The women whose work lives are documented here are on an occupational frontier and the social, psychological, and human implications of their presence is complicated and multidimensional. It is not enough to see them as "first women." The label "tokenizes" them and stops further understanding. It is time instead to assess how each woman has changed since her original integration, why dropout rates are still high, what employers are doing to make a success out of sexual integration, and what they have learned from their failures. This literature suggests also that environmental harassment toward women is now being identified and will eventually be eliminated through institutional reforms.[14]

Overview of Findings

This research has uncovered unexpected commonalities between women in different social classes and job types and it has revealed significant differences in the experiences of black and white women in nontraditional fields.[15] It has also uncovered an absence of attention to lesbian workplace issues. These findings suggest an agenda for action. It is time for someone to design a project focusing exclusively on women's work issues that arise out of differences in class, race, and sexual preference. Such a study would surely uncover publishing by small presses to which I did not have access.

The literature contains significant evidence, amassed over more than twenty years, of overadaptation by women to bad working conditions so that they could at least be in their field of choice.[16] There is evidence that gender consciousness is a critical issue for women in nontraditional fields, but that "coming out" in the workplace as a woman who has a right to a separate personhood from the culture of men is a psychological task that only the most resilient and brave have been able to accomplish.[17]

There is also a convincing body of evidence that documents intense, private stress and anxiety in women working in nontraditional occupations as diverse as that of fire fighter,[18] financial executive,[19] psychiatrist,[20] and student in a previously all-male university.[21] At this time the literature does not reflect that the causes of this stress are entirely understood by the women themselves, the people with whom they work, or other interested groups in American society. Overall, I uncovered no evidence of any research to suggest that there is a group identity shared by women in nontraditional fields, but I still wonder. There is significant evidence in the quotes from women in many fields that denial of discrimination and the effects of tokenism is a survival technique that some women use. As a response to a painful environment, personal distancing from real feelings takes place. This distancing effectively anesthetizes anxiety, but it also impedes growth and creativity. There is also evidence of tension between the acquired, workplace identity and the identity of private life.[22] All of these psychological issues demand further attention from women, clinicians, and researchers. This unaddressed pain deserves legitimation and, where possible, treatment and relief.

The naïveté of employers regarding the dynamics of sexual integration comes through as a significant theme in this literature. It is clear that while society at large may accept the idea that women can do equal work, individual attitudes of supervisors and coworkers take far longer to change and some men and women will never believe in equality deep down in their hearts.[23] A small body of literature emerged during this study that documented that some employers have developed strategies for avoiding temporary pitfalls or outright failures of sexual integration in their workplaces and these sources of information are highly important for other open-minded employers to read and evaluate as institutions change to adapt to a gender-coordinated society.

The literature gives evidence of real tensions between women in nontraditional fields and what they perceive as the women's movement. Paradoxical behavior, such as being a pioneer at work while remaining a tentative observer of women's liberation, is frequently documented. One researcher, studying the world of politics, has discovered what she calls the "closet feminist syndrome."[24] This may be what some women in nontraditional fields struggle with as they establish their careers by demonstrating their mastery over the content of the job, whatever it is.[25]

I have concluded, based on this research to date, that equal opportunity to apply for and get a high-paying job does not represent the breakthrough for women that has been so broadly publicized. While nontraditional or male-intensive work does improve women's financial status and still holds great hope for the future, the social dynamics of the integrated workplaces are often highly restrictive for women. Significant attitudinal and behavioral barriers against women must be broken in classrooms and workplaces if women are to achieve job security, advancement, and personal satisfaction in their nontraditional work.

A woman needs equality of opportunity in all phases of her career development, and at present it is not uniformly available. Such equality includes fair training opportunities as she learns the special aspects of her job, inclusion in informal communication networks, incentives and promotional opportunities, and a substantial career ladder. Subtle barriers at all stages of development exist where women have never worked before, and naïveté governs both employee and employer regarding the dynamics of sexual integration and strategies for removing these barriers.

Furthermore, women are beginning to see their right to "full personhood" in the workplace. They are starting to be less tolerant of unacceptable working conditions, and they are questioning their assimilation into a male culture. This differentiation is encouraging. A full flowering of their talents and contributions as women has become a new goal. But the women who are beginning to have these insights are still too few in number, and assimilation remains a dominant behavior pattern among women who integrate male fields.[26]

To end the tragic waste of talent and the undifferentiated identity that the assimilated woman represents, policy decisions making changes in government, business, and educational settings where women are employed or trained for nontraditional fields are indicated. In colleges and universities across the nation where women are educated to become, for example, surgeons, physicists, chemists, engineers, and orchestral conductors, broad-minded academic advising, appropriate women's advising, and, where possible, appropriate women's studies coursework must be integrated into the curricula. Continuing education courses on the changing mores regarding relationships between men and women in the workplace, communication skills between men and women, and sex-role stereotyping, among other relevant subjects, must be developed for alumni and others who return after a few years of work experience as seasoned veterans and when the pressure of initial degree preparation is over. In the workplace, evaluation instruments and personnel policies must be revised in light of new findings regarding the tokenism of women in nontraditional jobs. Supplementary training opportunities must be given equitably, and tracking of women into feminized or generally unpopular aspects of the field must be discouraged. Furthermore, women need to be included in informal communication networks so they too can have the inside information critical to security, promotion, satisfaction, and overall success.

Another implication of this research is that women's studies researchers, career and vocational educators, and other educators are often separated by wide gaps in understanding of each other's significant achievements in publishing and program initiatives. Bringing them together through conferences or other methods to learn from each other and ultimately to strengthen career and job education for women wherever it takes place is a critical developmental step that must happen in the future. Sex bias in career and job counseling must be eliminated.

Finally, new forms of education for work must be devised. As early as fifth or sixth grade, girls and their parents must begin to learn not only about nonsexist career options but also about the current realities of the American workplace for women. New intervention strategies in the public schools and in other educational settings such as churches and community organizations regarding work choices are essential if girls are to learn how to make effective and intelligent decisions by the time they graduate from high school in order to avoid sex-typed job choices. Policies to bring university and secondary-school educators together in collective projects to strengthen the preparation of high-school girls and college women for the realities of their future workplaces is another implication of this research.

The importance of these findings, coupled with the popular misconception that the mere presence of women in nontraditional fields represents progress, demonstrates the urgency of communicating these findings. Decision makers need to know the background of these conclusions and need to reach conclusions of their own regarding the meaning of the literature in order to develop effective policies and reform. There is a need for innovative programs of outreach efforts to disseminate this information to advance social progress.

Notes

1. Alvin Shuster, *New York Times,* 15 December 1961, p. 34, col. 3.

2. Ann Richards, Keynote Address to the Democratic National Convention, July 1988, in *Vital Speeches of the Day* 54 (1988):647. The inclusion of this quotation was suggested by my friend Judith Stitzel.

3. President's Commission on the Status of Women, *American Women* (Washington, D.C.: U.S. Government Printing Office, 1963).

4. Patricia G. Zelman, *Women, Work, and National Policy: The Kennedy-Johnson Years* (Ann Arbor, Mich.: University Microfilms International Research Press, 1980).

5. *American Women,* 1963.

6. *American Women,* 1963.

7. *American Women,* 1963.

8. Joseph Nathan Kane, *Famous First Facts: A Record of First Happenings, Discoveries, and Inventions in American History* (New York: H. W. Wilson Co., 1981).

9. J. Oliver Curwood, "The Girl Diver of the Great Lakes," *Women's Home Companion,* June 1905, pp. 16-17.

10. Brigid O'Farrell and Sharon Harlan, "Craftworkers and Clerks: The Effect of Male Co-Workers' Hostility on Women's Satisfactions with Non-Traditional Jobs," *Social Problems* 29, no. 3:252-65.

11. Judy Klemesrud, "Women Hammer Away at Male Job Bastions," *New York Times,* 22 November 1972, p. 42c.

12. U.S. Department of Commerce, Bureau of the Census, *Detailed Occupation of the Experienced Civilian Labor Force by Sex for the United States and Regions, 1980 and 1970, Supplementary Report,* Ser. PC 80-51-15 (Washington, D.C.: U.S. Government Printing Office, 1984).

13. Irene W. Hecht, "From the Desk of the President," *Wells College Express* 5, no. 3 (November 1989):4-5.

14. Pat Nyhan, "The Women of BIW (Bath Iron Works)," *Maine Times,* 10 November 1980, pp. 8-12.

15. Ann Kathleen Burlew, "The Experiences of Black Females in Traditional and Non-Traditional Professions," *Psychology of Women Quarterly* 6, no. 3 (Spring 1982):12-26.

16. Elaine Pitt Enarson, *Woods-Working Women: Sexual Integration in the U. S. Forest Service* (Tuscaloosa: University of Alabama Press, 1985).

17. Harriet G. Lerner, *Dance of Intimacy* (New York: Harper & Row, 1989).

18. Enarson, *Woods-Working Women.*

19. Patricia McBroom, *The Third Sex: The New Professional Woman* (New York: William Morrow & Co., 1986).

20. Beulah Parker, *Evolution of a Psychiatrist: Memoirs of a Woman Doctor* (New Haven: Yale University Press, 1987).

21. Janet Lever and Pepper Schwartz, *Women at Yale: Liberating a College Campus* (Indianapolis: Bobbs-Merrill Co., 1971).

22. McBroom, *The Third Sex.*

23. William A. Kahn and Faye Crosby, "Discriminating between Attitudes and Discriminatory Behaviors: Changes and Stasis," in *Women and Work: An Annual Review,* vol. 1, ed. Laurie Larwood, Ann H. Stromberg, and Barbara A. Gutek (Beverly Hills, Calif.: Sage Publications, 1985).

24. S. J. Carroll, "Women Candidates and Support for Feminist Concerns: The Closet Feminist Syndrome," *Western Political Quarterly* 37 (June 1984):307-323.

25. Jean Reith Schroedel, *Alone in a Crowd* (Philadelphia: Temple University Press, 1985).

26. Carolyn G. Heilbrun, *Reinventing Womanhood* (New York: W.W. Norton & Co., 1979), 46.

Basic Reference Sources Consulted

Any skillful bibliographer recognizes reference sources as important tools to use in effective research. In this section, I want to give credit to the women's studies bibliographers and other researchers who have gone before me to create compelling cognitive maps to emerging areas of new understanding in writing and scholarship about women. Their work advanced mine, and I am grateful to them and their invaluable reference publications.

According to Patricia Ballou's *Women: A Bibliography of Bibliographies* (Boston: G.K. Hall & Co., 1986), there are four bibliographical studies on the subject of women in nontraditional occupations. The most recent of these, Merri-Ann Cooper et al., *Introduction of Women into Work Groups in Traditionally Male Career Fields: Annotated Bibliography* (Bethesda, Md.: Advanced Research Resources Organization, 1980) includes 114 citations and is thirty-one pages long. The most comprehensive source on the subject is over ten years old: Koba Associates, *Women in Nontraditional Occupations: A Bibliography* (Washington, D.C.: U.S. Office of Education, 1976). This was preceded by *Dimensions of Women's Employment in Nontraditional Female Occupations: A Selected Bibliography* (Washington, D.C.: U.S. Office of Education, 1975) by Martha Wingard Tack and Deborah Taylor Ashford. A fourth, narrowly constructed study is Jeanne Parr Lemkau's "Personality and Background Characteristics of Women in Male-Dominated Professions," *Psychology of Women Quarterly* 5 (Winter 1979): 221-40, which includes only forty-two citations. All of these sources are dated and the comprehensive ones are seriously so. This bibliographical study is current, more comprehensive, and national in scope in its subject analysis. I have not included the citations mentioned in the works above in a comprehensive fashion. Serious researchers will need to use their works and mine together.

Beyond these sources of information, my work was advanced greatly by the work of scholars whose monographs, articles, or essays contained serious bibliographical analysis. I have chosen to include these references in the text of the appropriate section of the book, and where they are relevant I have marked them accordingly.

1   Abbott, Linda M. C. "Women, Work, and Self-Esteem: A Bibliographic Essay." *Choice* (October 1987):265-74.
　　　Abbott's essay is an excellent piece of work. She asks some probing questions about the individual woman's response to her society that promotes such conflicting attitudes toward women in the workplace. Then she discusses the literature of women at work and their self-concepts, mentioning 125 current books in the process. She presents in-depth bibliographical analysis throughout the essay.

2   Ballou, Patricia K. *Women: A Bibliography of Bibliographies.* Boston: G. K. Hall & Co., 1980.
　　　A landmark study; indispensable. Ballou cites the Koba Associates bibliography as well as the Tack and Ashford study.

3   Ballou, Patricia K. *Women: A Bibliography of Bibliographies.* 2d ed. Boston: G. K. Hall & Co., 1986.
　　　The new edition cites two recently discovered bibliographies on women at work in nontraditional fields as well as the two mentioned in the first edition.

4   Capek, Mary Ellen S. "Women's Information Online: The Work of the National Council for Research on Women." *Feminist Collections: A Quarterly of Women's Studies Resources* 8, no. 3 (Spring 1987):8-10.
　　　Second half of article begun in Winter 1986 issue (see below) on the information projects of the National Council for Research on Women.

5   Capek, Mary Ellen S. "Women's Language: The Work of the National Council for Research on Women." *Feminist Collections: A Quarterly of Women's Studies Resources* 8, no. 2 (Winter 1986):6-10.
　　　Capek discusses behind-the-scenes work involved in creating the *Women's Thesaurus.*

6   Capek, Mary Ellen S. *A Women's Thesaurus: An Index of Language Used to Describe and Locate Information by and about Women.* New York: Harper & Row, 1987.

Many of the "freetext" terms defined in Capek's work have been used in this book's index.

7   Cooper, Merri-Ann, Imhoff, David L., and Myers, David C. *Introduction of Women into Work Groups in Traditionally Male Career Fields: Annotated Bibliography.* Bethesda, Md.: Advanced Research Research Resources Organization, 1980, 31 pp. ED188 012.

This 114-item annotated bibliography is a survey of research findings on the individual, group, and organizational factors involved in the introduction of women into work groups in traditionally male fields. The authors comment that "most of the research reviewed is concerned with identifying rather than alleviating problems that women experience in nontraditional careers." There is heavy emphasis on integration by women of the armed services, and it should be noted that the creation of this source was sponsored by the Air Force Human Resources Laboratory at Brooks Air Force Base in Texas.

8   Davis, A. B. *Bibliography on Women with Special Emphasis on Their Roles in Science and Society.* New York: Science History Publications, 1974.

Compiled from selected books and articles from the *Library of Congress Catalogue: A Cumulative List of Works* from 1950 through March 1973. Some entries deal with women's employment in nontraditional occupations.

9   Farr, Sidney Saylor. *Appalachian Women: An Annotated Bibliography.* Lexington: University of Kentucky Press, 1981.

References to women and work in the Appalachian region are relevant. Farr cites more than twenty-five articles on women coal miners and also includes citations to many accounts throughout the book's thirteen sections of the educational and employment rights activism of Appalachian women.

10   *Feminist Periodicals: A Current Listing of Contents 1981-.* Quarterly. Madison: University of Wisconsin.

A current awareness service. Nonscholarly and popular titles are included. Work is a frequent topic; nontraditional work is discussed less frequently, but the topic certainly occurs often enough to be useful to this study.

11   Gilbert, Victor Francis, and Tatla, Darshan Singh, comps. *Women's Studies: A Bibliography of Dissertations 1870-1982.* New York: Basil Blackwell, 1985.
        Women's employment issues are treated in some of the dissertations.

12   Haber, Barbara. *Women in America, A Guide to Books 1963-1975.* Urbana-Champaign: University of Illinois Press, 1978.
        An insightful introduction to both emerging issues in publishing about women and individual books of substantial interest.

13   Hady, Maureen E., et al. *Women's Periodicals and Newspapers from the 18th Century to 1981: A Union List of the Holdings of Madison, Wisconsin, Libraries.* Edited by James P. Danky. Boston: G. K. Hall & Co., 1982.

14   Hoffman, Nancy, and Howe, Florence, eds. *Women Working: An Anthology of Stories and Poems.* Old Westbury, N.Y.: Feminist Press, 1979.
        More than half the selections treat women's unpaid work. The editors include a short story by Rikki Lights, a black physician. It describes her periodic rage in medical school in reaction to the discrimination she experienced.

15   Interdepartmental Committee on the Status of Women. *American Women, 1963-1968.* Washington, D.C.: U.S. Government Printing Office, 1968.
        Factual accounts of progress since 1963 when the first "American Women" report was offered to the president. (An executive order established this interdepartmental committee of cabinet members and a citizen's advisory council of private citizens to ensure the continued advancement of the status of women.)

16   Kramarae, Cheris, and Treichler, Paula A. *A Feminist Dictionary: In Our Own Words*. Boston: Pandora Press, 1985.
        A wonderful reference book, totally iconoclastic.

17   Lerner, Gerda. *Women Are History: Bibliography in the History of American Women*. 4th rev. ed. Madison: University of Wisconsin, Graduate Program in Women's History. 1986.
        Not annotated, but full of important, first-rate work. There are 1,358 citations in 1986 edition. Available from the Graduate Program in Women's History, University of Wisconsin-Madison, Department of History, 3211 Humanities Bldg., 455 North Park Street, Madison, WI 53706.

18   Loeb, Catherine R., Searing, Susan E., and Stineman, Esther. *Women's Studies: A Core List of Significant Works, 1980-1985*. Englewood, Colo.: Libraries Unlimited, 1986.
        The most comprehensive analysis ever written of women's studies resources that are in print and appropriate for an academic library. It was built on the foundation laid by Esther Stineman's *Women's Studies: A Recommended Core Bibliography*, 1979.

19   McIntyre, Janet A. *Women and Employment: A Select Annotated Bibliography*. Wellington, New Zealand: Committee on Women, 1978.
        McIntyre's 314-entry bibliography, published at the New Zealand Library School during the diploma course of 1977, is a thirty-seven-page pamphlet. The sections on vocations, trade unions, retraining, and management are of particular relevance to this study.

20   Millman, Marcia, and Kanter, Rosabeth Moss. *Another Voice: Feminist Perspectives on Social Life and Social Science*. New York: Anchor Books, 1975.
        Carolyn Sachs comments in her introduction to *The Invisible Farmers* (see entry 567) that the book above "discusses and defends the value of qualitative research that allows women to speak for themselves so that one can understand their subjective experiences."

21   Paramore, Katherine. *Nontraditional Job Training for Women: A Bibliography and a Resource Directory for Employment and Training Planners.* Chicago: Council of Planning Librarians Bibliographies.

Based on author's master's thesis entitled "Planning Nontraditional Job Training Programs for Women: A Guide to CETA Planners and Program Operators." Available from the author at Operation Analysis Division Office and Field Operations and Monitoring Office of Community Planning and Development, Department of Housing and Urban Development, Washington, D.C. 20410.

22   Phelps, Ann T., Farmer, Helen S., and Backer, Thomas E. *New Career Options for Women: A Selected Annotated Bibliography.* New York: Human Sciences Press, 1977.

A total of 240 books, journal articles, and government reports were selected for this bibliography based on statistical soundness, adequate controls for sources of variance, fair representation of occupational groups, and sampling for varying demographic groups. The titles noted by Phelps et al. are not repeated in this book.

The authors include chapters on women at work in the 1970s in many areas: internationally; in the United States; in part-time jobs; in the crafts; and in management positions. They also discuss women's opportunities in training and education, the working mother's impact on her children, biological differences between women and men, and the issue of achievement motivation and psychological differences between the sexes. They emphasize career counseling theories and concepts for women and include sources of information for special groups of women. They also include sections in the bibliography on sex bias and counseling and on counseling techniques.

23   Rossi, Alice. "Equality between the Sexes: An Immodest Proposal." *Daedalus* 93, no. 2 (Spring 1964):607-652.

Rossi asserts a claim for "sex equality." She defines this as "a socially androgynous conception of the roles of men and women, in which they are equal and similar in spheres such as intellectual, artistic, political, and occupational interests and preparation and complementary only in those spheres dictated by physiological differences between the sexes." Written in 1964, this essay calls for expanding the "common ground on which men and women base their lives together by changing the social defractions of approved characteristics and behavior for both sexes." Later published in a 1967 book called *The Woman in America,* edited by Robert Jay Lifton (Boston: Beacon Press, 1967), this essay is firmly established as a classic of feminist thought, according to Barbara Haber, curator of printed books at the Schlesinger Library on the History of Women in America and a noted authority on woman's studies. It is well worth reviewing in light of the context of this book's consideration of women at work in nontraditional fields.

24 Schlesinger Library on the History of Women in America. *The Manuscript Inventories and the Catalog of Manuscripts, Books, and Periodicals.* 2d ed. 10 vols. Boston: G. K. Hall & Co., 1984.
      This set provides access to the retrospective collections within the nation's richest collection of works on women.

25 Searing, Susan E., ed. *New Books on Women and Feminism.* Semiannual (1979-). Madison: University of Wisconsin.
      Available from Women's Studies Librarian, 112A Memorial Library, 728 State St., Madison, WI 53706.

26 Searing, Susan E., and Shult, Linda. *Feminist Collections: A Quarterly of Wisconsin Resources.* Madison: University of Wisconsin, 1980.
      Consulted as source for interlibrary loans during the research process.

27 Sullivan, Kaye. *Films for, by, and about Women.* Metuchen, N.J.: Scarecrow Press, 1980.
      An excellent reference book on films, with many citations for both traditional and nontraditional films on women at work.

28 Tack, Martha Wingard, and Ashford, Deborah Taylor. *Dimensions of Women's Employment in Non-Traditional Female Occupations: A Selected Bibliography, January 1970-1975.* Washington, D.C.: U.S. Office of Education, Bureau of Occupational and Adult Education, 1975.
      A comprehensive bibliography covering five important years of publishing on the subject of women at work in nontraditional fields.

29   Williamson, Jane. *New Feminist Scholarship: A Guide to Bibliographies*. Old Westbury, N.Y.: Feminist Press, 1979.
Must be used with Ballou's work, cited in entries 2 and 3.

30   Williamson, Jane, et al., eds. *Women's Action Almanac: A Complete Resource Guide*. New York: Morrow, 1979.
This book, compiled by the Women's Action Alliance, has a useful chapter on career development for women.

31   *Women, 1965-1975*. Glen Rock, N.J.: Microfilming Corporation of America, 1978.
One-volume coverage of the *New York Times*'s publishing on women for one decade.

32   *Women's Annual*. Boston: G. K. Hall & Co., 1980-85.
All five years of this annual contain bibliographical essays on women and work, and all are relevant for researchers using this book, as few of the publications mentioned in those articles could be repeated here. The last, published in 1985 in the *Women's Annual* no. 5, focuses specifically on women at work in nontraditional fields.

Women at Work in Nontraditional Fields –
General Sources of Information

Women doing "men's work" are still very rare, of course, but when pioneers do move into traditionally male jobs they challenge important barriers. These first steps are important, not because they open new horizons for a privileged few – and they do – but because they are part of a larger, more complex process of change. We live in a world rigidly stratified by gender, so strikingly evident in the labor force, where four of every five women work in white- and pink-collar ghettos of the female work world. Indeed the trend is toward increasing sex segregation at work.

–Elaine Pitt Enarson,
*Woods-Working Women:
Sexual Integration in the
U.S. Forest Service*, 1984

This twenty-five-year overview shows that the literature was sparse during the first ten years of the study, but the body of work increased dramatically by the mid-1970s. The early writing tended to treat the nonconforming working woman as a bit of a freak. This attitude persisted well into the 1980s, and it may never disappear entirely. Fortunately, that literature – both popular and scholarly – is balanced by substantially increased understanding by authors of the dynamics of the sex-segregated workplace.

33   Abir-Am, Pnina G., and Outram, Dorinda, eds. *Uneasy Careers and Intimate Lives: Women in Science 1789-1979.* Foreword by Margaret Rossiter. Douglass Series on Women's Lives and the Meaning of Gender. New Brunswick, N.J.: Rutgers University Press, 1987.

9

This book contains twelve detailed case studies of pioneering and outstanding women whose lives as scientists were complicated by the difficult intersections between their personal lives and their professional careers. Each woman's life is scrupulously documented with full attention to primary source material. Attempts are made to expose reasons for the exclusion of the domestic realm from previous historical considerations of science. The institutionalization of science is discussed in order to explain its effect on the developing careers of women scientists, particularly between the two world wars. In the introduction, the editors discuss various themes uniting the essays, including the very real suffering the women experienced as a result of "complex, ongoing and consistent processes of social and intellectual marginalization." One of the many strengths of the book is its international focus.

34   Adams, Major Jerome. *Report of the Admission of Women to the U.S. Military Academy (Project Athena III).* West Point, N.Y.: United States Military Academy at West Point, Department of Behavioral Sciences and Leadership, June 1979, 236 pp.

In 1975, study of the performance of women as cadets at West Point began. It was called Project Athena and the program conducted longitudinal research to assess how well women were being integrated into the corps of cadets. In this monograph, readers will find data derived from surveys, interviews, informal experiments, direct observations, and archival records about the year 1978-79. The report concludes that "progress is being made toward the goal of the full assimilation of women." The report covers admissions, cadet basic training, field training, and advanced training. Just the fact that they were promoting "assimilation" is discouraging, however.

35   Anczarki, Susan J., ed. *The Women's Directory (N.J.).* 3d ed. Trenton, N.J.: NOW, Women's Rights Task Force on Education, 1975, 11 pp.

A roster of women employed in nontraditional female occupations for use by schools, colleges, and others concerned with career counseling.

36   Anderson, Rosemarie. "Motive to Avoid Success: A Profile." *Sex Roles* 4 (1978):239-48.

Presents results of study, which showed that female college students in their first year who aspired to a male-dominated occupation did not fear success.

The analyses reported in this paper are based on responses to five items in a 1967 American Council on Education survey of first-time, full-time college freshmen. National normative summaries were reported. The sample contained 186,000 students attending 252 representative institutions of higher education.

In a series of studies of this data, comparisons were made between self-descriptions of college women whose stories contained "motive to avoid success" imagery with women whose stories did not contain such imagery. The women who did not exhibit "motive to avoid success" were found to be more likely to choose atypical careers and to have mothers who had also made that choice.

37   Appelbaum, L. R. "The Female Occupational Selection Process: Atypicality of Occupational Choice." Ph.D. dissertation, University of Illinois at Champaign, 1980.

38   Ashburn, Elizabeth A. *Motivation, Personality, and Work-Related Characteristics of Women in Male-Dominated Professions.* Ruth Strang Research Award Monograph Series, no. 2. Washington, D.C.: National Association for Women Deans, Administrators, and Counselors, 1977, 32 pp.

When she wrote this monograph, the author was studying for her Ph.D. in educational psychology, a male-dominated field, at the State University of New York at Buffalo. The work is an important literature review and analysis. Ashburn begins with a discussion of the presumed motivation in women for selecting nontraditional fields. She considers the personality and socialization of women who have chosen male-dominated professions. She finds these women strongly oriented toward achievement; but this drive is complicated by several variables including the degree of the fear of success, the degree of need for affiliation, and the strength of the individual's internalized stereotype of the feminine image. She also thinks an important factor in a woman's motivation for choosing a nontraditional professional career is her drive for autonomy. In her discussion of personality she clearly states this theory: "The prevalent stereotypic personality of women in male-dominated professions is if they are normal women they are abnormal people; while if they are normal people with ordinary technical interests and capabilities, they are abnormal women." In an important section of her analysis, Ashburn considers women's "aloofness" from other women and their relationships with men in the workplace. In the conclusion, Ashburn calls for more change in the orientation of career development and counseling theory and research. She calls for counselors to deal with multiple-role conflicts by helping to maximize individual development rather than "guiding women automatically to acceptance of career goals as secondary." Overall this is an interesting assessment of the relevant literature as of 1976 about women in nontraditional professions.

39   Association of American Colleges. Project on the Status and Education of Women. *Nontraditional Careers.* Reprinted from *On Campus with Women.* Washington, D.C.: Association of American Colleges, Spring 1981, 16 pp.

40   Association of American Colleges. Project on the Status and Education of Women. *Recruiting Women for Traditionally "Male" Careers: Programs and Resources for Getting Women into the Men's World.* Washington, D.C.: Association of American Colleges, October 1977, 9 pp.

41   Astin, Helen S. "Factors Associated with the Participation of Women Doctorates in the Labor Force." *Personnel and Guidance Journal* 46, no. 3 (November 1967):240-46.
        Astin explored work histories of 1,547 women who earned doctorates in 1957 and 1958. She wanted to know the personal and environmental factors that were associated with the labor force participation of these women in the late 1960s. She found that a high percentage of the women who earned doctorates in 1957 and 1958 were in the labor force. But the greatest loss of talent was in the natural sciences where 18 percent dropped out of the labor force. She reports extensively on 28 variables in personal and family background and 19 variables in the women's environmental experiences.

42   Banas, Casey. "More Women Eye 'Male' Careers." *Boston Globe,* 7 February 1981, p. 7.

An article about the fifteenth annual survey of entering freshmen conducted by Alexander Astin of UCLA and the American Council on Education, which found that about 27 percent of freshmen women in a sample numbering 291,491 were planning a career in business, law, medicine, or engineering.

43 Blank, S. "An Investigation of Personality Variables of Female Junior College Students Choosing Male- and Female-Dominated Careers." Ph.D. dissertation, University of Miami, 1974.

44 Bridges, Judith S., and Bower, Mary S., eds. "The Effects of Perceived Job Availability for Women on College Women's Attitudes toward Prestigious Male-Dominated Occupations." *Psychology of Women Quarterly* 9 (June 1985):265-76.

Bridges and Bower studied 219 introductory psychology students who were women. They hypothesized "that college women's expectations about and interest in high-prestige male-dominated occupations would be most positive when they perceived the occupations as providing good opportunities for women, and would be most negative when they perceived the opportunities as poor." They investigated the effects of sex-role orientation on the evaluation of prestigious occupations in perceived opportunities for women. They found that the women were influenced by their perception of an occupation's sex-related job availability. Women were interested in fields where they thought there were opportunities for them, but they found a dilemma: it was unlikely that a perception of good opportunities would occur in prestigious occupations because the prestigious occupations were dominated by men. The college women surveyed expected prestigious occupations to provide the highest levels of intellectual stimulation and the greatest degree of approval from others. The authors conclude that sex-role orientation is related to aspects of career decision making and career choice, and they recommend further research in the future.

45 Brudnez, Juliet. "Attracting Women to New Fields." *Boston Globe,* 8 March 1984, pp. 45-46.

Brudnez discusses ten years of integration by women of male-dominated professional careers but states that blue-collar occupations have not caught on as well. She cites some reasons for this, but she also thinks prospects are good for the future because resources have been developed to help schools and employers recruit and train female candidates.

46   Brudnez, Juliet. "Sex Stereotyping of Jobs Still the Norm." *Boston Globe,* 26 December 1982.

   A brief article surveying the many opportunities for women in nontraditional jobs and listing some schools and offices to contact for further information.

47   Career Planning Center. *A Non-Traditional Look at Women: A Guide for Management.* Los Angeles: Career Planning Center, 1977.

   This booklet was put together by members of the Governor's Task Force on Nontraditional Employment for Women in 1976 in cooperation with the Career Planning Center, Inc., after Governor Edmund G. Brown, Jr., of California awarded them a grant to develop methods and demonstrate new techniques leading to industry/employer acceptance of women in nontraditional jobs. It is a detailed guide for employers, covering: definitions of nontraditional work for women; barriers to successful employment; management, recruitment, and motivation of women; encouragement of peers' acceptance of women's integration; legal definition of equal employment opportunities; and other pertinent subjects. The Career Planning Center, Inc., has substantial experience in these areas; in 1972 the Center established a nonprofit tax-exempt community agency dedicated to expansion of women's career potential and women's economic independence.

   This publication is interesting and useful for several reasons. First, it explains the Employer's Task Force, which is comprised of thirty major Los Angeles companies that offer unusual opportunities for women ranging from nontraditional entertainment careers to computer-science jobs. The task force researched whether barriers existed, defined them, actively sought ways to explode myths about women, examined unrealistic job descriptions, and developed solutions to sexist labeling. Second, the book begins with a management checklist for moving women into nontraditional jobs. It includes: benefits; sources of qualified women; EEO implications; recruiting; outreach; interviewing and counseling; internal and external programs; barriers/problems and solutions; feedback system/measures. Each item in the list is discussed in detail. Finally, the book identifies twenty-six barriers to successful employment of women in nontraditional fields, with suggestions for eliminating the barrier and the benefit to the organization.

Employers wanting to be responsive to women integrating their workplaces would be well advised to have a look at this booklet. It is available from the Career Planning Center, 1623 South La Cienaga Boulevard, Los Angeles, CA 90035.

48 Cauley, Constance Drake. *Time for a Change: A Woman's Guide to Nontraditional Occupations.* Cambridge, Mass.: Ellis Associates, 1981.

A discussion of new work opportunities for women.

49 Center for the Study, Education, and Advancement of Women. University of California, Berkeley. *Women and Work in the 1980's: Perspectives from the 1930's and 1940's: Proceedings of a Conference Held May 14, 1981, at the University of California, Berkeley.* 1981, 155 pp.

Papers about women's work in the Great Depression, child care during the Second World War, job segregation during the 1940s, and other pertinent issues.

50 "City to Recruit Women to Six Job Categories." *Crain's Chicago Business,* 12 May 1986.

Announces that the city of Chicago will implement a pilot program to recruit women into nontraditional jobs. They include truck driver, bridge tender, tree trimmer, laborer, stationary firer, and lamp maintenance worker. (A stationary firer is a person who tends to the maintenance of boilers.)

51 Coffin, Fai, and Mintier, Judy. "A Woman Can Do a Man's Job." *Tradeswoman* 6, no. 1 (Winter 1986-87):16-19.

A revealing discussion by women on the front lines.

52 Crawford, J. D. "Career Development and Career Choice in Pioneer and Traditional Women." *Journal of Vocational Behavior* 12 (1987): 129-39.

Based on his doctoral dissertation study of Texas Tech University, Crawford notes that college seniors designated as "pioneers" had better-educated mothers than did women who were designated as "traditionals." (The term "traditionals" refers to women who choose sex-typical jobs.) Crawford's data supports the theory developed by G. Psathas in 1968 regarding occupational choice for women. (G. Psathas, "Toward a Theory of Occupational Choice for Women," *Sociology and Social Research* 52:[1968]: 253-66.)

53   Crittenden, Ann. "Women Cite Neglect in U.S. Job Training." *New York Times,* 12 February 1979, p. D3.

Covers the fact that a number of prominent women's organizations are concerned that the Labor Department is doing very little to place women in traditionally male jobs. Wider Opportunities for Women, Inc., of Washington, D.C., pointed out in 1978 that only 1.4 percent of the Labor Department's budget went for programs specifically designed for women.

54   Cummings, Bernice, and Schuck, Victoria. *Women Organizing: An Anthology.* Metuchen, N.J.: Scarecrow Press, 1979.

Has a section on women in nontraditional careers.

55   Diamond, H. H. "Suicide by Women Professionals." Ph.D. dissertation, California School of Professional Psychology, 1977.

56   Dixon, B. L. B. "Competence Perceptions of Female Nontraditional Occupation Aspirants." Ph.D. dissertation, Florida State University, 1982.

57   Dolan, Carrie. "Success Stories: How Four Women Are Prospering in Jobs Usually Held by Men." *Wall Street Journal,* 29 June 1983, p. 1.

An ironworker, a bank executive, an astronaut, and a politician are interviewed and discussed.

58   Donahue, T. J. "Discrimination against Young Women in Career Selection by High School Counselors." Ph.D. dissertation, University of Michigan, 1976.

59   Duncan, Emily. "Nontraditional Occupations: A Study of Women Who Have Made the Choice." *Vocational Guidance Quarterly,* March 1985, pp. 241-48.

While describing a sound study with fascinating results, the article's authors also provide thorough bibliographical references to other studies regarding the issues of women in nontraditional employment. The study describes information reported by women who have chosen occupations in skilled crafts, labor, and technical fields. The authors wanted to provide women with information regarding both barriers and facilitators in nontraditional jobs. The sample included seventy-five women, representing approximately 25 percent of the tradeswomen in the Seattle, Washington, area.

60   Ehrhart, Julie Kahn, and Sandler, Bernice R. *Looking for More Than a Few Good Women in Traditionally Male Fields.* Washington, D.C.: Project on the Status and Education of Women, Association of American Colleges, January 1987.

A twenty-four-page report that thoroughly explores the underrepresentation of women in programs or disciplines considered nontraditional such as engineering, agricultural sciences, computer and information sciences. The report focuses on the dynamics of nontraditional fields in higher education. It explores reasons why women do not pursue degrees in nontraditional fields in greater numbers, and it addresses many actions institutions can take to improve the overall situation. In addition to compelling insights, the report offers extensive bibliographical references and an "institutional self-evaluation checklist."

61   Eko, M. J. "Factors Influencing Women's Choices of Industrial Technical Education in Arizona Community Colleges." Ed.D. dissertation, Arizona State University, 1980.

62   Enarson, Elaine Pitt. *Woods-Working Women: Sexual Integration in the U.S. Forest Service.* Tuscaloosa: University of Alabama Press, 1985.

This is one of the landmark books discovered during this study. Enarson creates a vivid portrait, as she says, "of women and men working together in the nation's forests where women are slowly integrating work crews and workplaces once exclusively male." Enarson explores in a personal way the private side of sexual integration. She investigates interaction and emotion at work through an analysis of the social structure of the details of everyday life in the politics of affirmative action, what it is like when women supervise men, the sexualization of the workplace, and overall patterns of change in the various formerly all-male occupations in the U.S. Forest Service. In her conclusion, Enarson raises the issue of women's challenge of the conditions for women in their nontraditional workplaces. She points out how firmly entrenched the traditions and customs of male privilege are, and she identifies male control mechanisms: sexualization of the workplace, including cultivation of sexual or quasisexual relations with women coworkers; sexual harassment and abuse; elaboration of a sexual division of labor ensuring male dominance; assertion of formal and informal authority thorough supervision and training; and definition of specific models of accommodation for women newcomers. The "determined women committed to an equitable future in forestry" are the challengers to male control. Enarson found that they used various techniques to challenge conditional acceptance, including: deemphasis on sexual themes at work; demonstration of competence and commitment; seeking male alliance and sponsorship; development of a repertoire of interpersonal tactics to control resistance; pursuit of organizational avenues of redress; and cultivation of formal and informal networks of support between women. But she goes on to assert that many women just accept limiting conditions as a compromise for having the job in the first place, and this acceptance of compromise guarantees the old order. She says "struggling over the terms of acceptance" is the essential task made more difficult because of tokenism. She suggests a long-term strategy for women of challenging boundaries in order to desegregate their workplaces completely.

63   Epstein, Cynthia Fuchs. "Positive Effects of the Multiple Negative: Explaining the Success of Black Professional Women." In *Changing Women in a Changing Society,* edited by J. Haber. Chicago: University of Chicago Press, 1973.

Epstein studied thirty-one black women in the professions of law, medicine, dentistry, university teaching, journalism, and public relations. She found that these women had high regard for each other and far less self-hatred than their white counterparts. She found that they did not doubt the competence of other women: they said they were happy to work with women colleagues because they were more reliable and more willing to work than some of the men they knew.

64 Epstein, Cynthia Fuchs. *Woman's Place: Options and Limits in Professional Careers.* Berkeley: University of California Press, 1971.

Long seen as a landmark book, Epstein's work is full of insights that are highly relevant to understanding the social dynamics for women of "men's professions." Her study focuses on law. Epstein divides her book into six chapters. They consider ideals, images, and ideology of women and of women's roles in American society; the socialization process in careers; reconciliation to women's roles; the characteristic structures of professions and how they affect women's participation in work; what the inside of professional life is like; and how professions themselves are changing in response to the new demands of women. Written in 1971 and now almost 20 years old, Epstein's conceptual framework for the issues of women in professions is still highly relevant to understanding the social dynamics of women in male-intensive fields to this day. The author includes an excellent bibliography of pertinent materials published in the 1960s.

65 Federation of Southern Cooperatives. Rural Women's Opportunity Center. *Placing Rural Minority Women in Training Situations for Nontraditional Jobs.* Newton, Mass.: Women's Educational Equity Act (WEEA) Publishing Center, 1979.

This ninety-four-page booklet discusses nontraditional training opportunities for rural minority women. It is available from the WEEA Publishing Center, 55 Chapel Street, Newton, MA 02160. Compiled by Alice Paris, Rural Women's Opportunity Center, Epes, Ala.

66 Friedan, Betty. *The Second Stage.* New York: Summit Books, 1981.

The fifth chapter of this book, entitled "Reality Test at West Point," 163-98, describes Friedan's participation in three days of lectures in 1980 at West Point. She was part of a new program on "American Institutions," and the West Point officials were interested in her views on the second stage of feminism because some of them were thinking along the same lines. She describes coming away from West Point liking and being impressed by the women cadets. She felt they had integrated a male bastion and retained their identities as women.

She felt they had quickly found that "core of strength in themselves" and were in good shape to face the challenges ahead. Overall, she found that West Point officials were making an attempt to break free of machismo, and she emerged with an optimistic sense of the military's future.

67   Goodman, Ellen. "New Ground for Women." *Boston Globe,* 17 September 1976.

In an editorial, Goodman suggests that there will always be a few hard-core resisters to the idea of women in unusual roles. But most everyone else will change attitudes as the facts of reality dictate. She suggests that official groups such as the House of Deputies of the Episcopal Church need to take a positive stand on the principle of women priests, and then she predicts that "public acceptance will do what it does best: follow." She comments further: "Many are opposed to women in 'men's roles' because they've never seen them, they've never tried them. They regard a woman priest with the suspicion normally directed at raw oysters. The prejudice remains unshakable as long as the experience is unchanged." Illustrating her points, she concludes: "The horrified alumni of Yale discovered after a few years that the sky did not fall over the female dorms of New Haven. The patrolmen of Washington who were opposed to buddying up with women largely accepted them a year later. The same people who couldn't tolerate the idea of a woman doctor went to Elizabeth Blackwell when they were sick. And West Point marches on."

68   Greenfield, S. T. "Attitudes toward Work and Success of Women Employed in Male- vs. Female-Dominated Jobs." D.B.A. dissertation, University of Southern California, 1978.

69   Hacker, Andrew. "Women vs. Men in the Work Force." *New York Times Magazine,* 9 December 1984, pp. 124-29.

Hacker discusses women's advances in nontraditional jobs and concludes that these developments are occurring at the expense of men. He states that "women will have to face the prospect of living with men they have outpaced."

70   Hannonen-Gladden, Helena Maria Anneli. "Stratification of
      Women in the American Labor Force: 1972-1982." Ph.D.
      dissertation, Brigham Young University, 1983.
          The author found that occupational distributions remained the
      same during the period studied. Women were concentrated for the full
      ten years in clerical, service, and professional/technical occupations.
      Gender-based income differentials also continued. The author outlines
      four issues that she thinks require further research: first, that equal
      employment laws have no effect on attitudes; second, that both men
      and women need to know more about the new kinds of jobs available to
      women; third, that we must know more about the relationship of status
      attainment and the influence of the mother; and fourth, that we need to
      modify the current status attainment methods.

71   Hart, Louisa G. *Wider Opportunities for Women Working for You: A
      Guide to Employing Women in Non-Traditional Jobs.* Washington,
      D.C.: Wider Opportunities for Women (WOW), 28 pp.
          For employers who wish to employ women equally. Mentions
      that WOW has worked for twelve years as a national organization
      committed to equal employment opportunities for women. They assist
      private and public employers with their specialized affirmative action
      needs. Takes employer through first steps, recruitment, the break-in
      period, and the long-term effects. Photos by Les Hienig and Martha
      Tabor.

72   Heilbrun, Carolyn G. *Reinventing Womanhood.* New York: W.W.
      Norton & Co., 1979.
          Heilbrun says in the opening chapter of this important book
      ("Personal and Prefatory") that she wants to examine the factors that
      make it possible for women to achieve what she calls "a position of
      autonomy in male-dominated worlds." She reveals that she is
      particularly interested in women who achieved their positions without
      receiving the support of other women and also without giving support
      to other women. She states that women of achievement in male-
      dominated fields have been able to earn acceptance only by being
      "honorary men" while simultaneously sacrificing their womanhood.
      The book discusses the contradictions and paradoxes inherent in her
      subjects' lives, which she recognizes and identifies with because of her
      own ultimately successful struggles to become a full professor at a
      major university. Much of her literary discussion and analysis is
      integrated with personal and autobiographical insights. Heilbrun is

angry at the women who become "honorary males" because she believes that they slow progress for other women. She condemns them and regards them as the enemy. This is a provocative book, but some of its ideas are disturbingly dated. It was written over ten years ago, and we understand a great deal more now about both the structural reasons for women's behavior in nontraditional fields and their own internal struggle with the effects of assimilation. With our recently accumulated knowledge it seems more to the point to offer understanding to these women instead of distancing and condemning them. The categorical generalizations Heilbrun makes in this book impede the opening of new channels of communication among women and between women and men.

73   Hobson, G. L. "Anxiety in Women Associated with a Nontraditional or Traditional Career Choice." Ph.D. dissertation, University of Oklahoma, 1982.

74   Holsendolph, Ernest. "U.S. Moves to Require Contractors to Hire Women on Federal Jobs." *New York Times,* 11 August 1977, pp. 1, 36.
        An announcement that the proposed regulations will be available for comment is made here, and the fact that the Building Trades Council of the American Federation of Labor and the Congress of Industrial Organizations are sure to oppose them is also mentioned. Holsendolph quotes the Labor Department's report that accompanies the draft of the regulations: "Women are often discouraged from even considering skilled trades as a viable source of employment because of views about 'women's roles.' By rule and by practice young girls are excluded from such courses as auto shop, drafting, and wood shop, and tracked into the so-called 'women's work courses' such as home economics and typing."

75   Illinois State Board of Education. Department of Adult Vocational and Technical Education. Research and Development Section. *New Pass: Nontraditional Education for Women, Paths to Economic Self-Sufficiency.* Chicago: Women Employed Institute, July 1986.
        A life planning/career awareness/nontraditional job options curriculum for economically disadvantaged teenaged mothers. This 14-

week curriculum was funded by the Women Employed Institute, Suite 415, 5 S. Wabash, Chicago, IL 60603.

76   Jacobson, Aileen. *Women in Charge: Dilemmas of Women in Authority.* New York: Van Nostrand Reinhold Co., 1985.

Jacobson describes some of the problems that women have as authority figures by looking at the histories of women who have had greater or lesser success in dealing with their own work circumstances. She also offers suggestions for solving some of those problems. She shares findings from thirty-five interviews with women all over America in education, business, and the arts. The author offers advice on the following problems: developing assertive behavior; balancing human needs with corporate demands; promoting comfortable working relationships without losing authority; giving and receiving criticism; dealing effectively with sexual harassment; displaying expertise to gain favorable recognition without creating destructive jealousy; overcoming stereotypical expectations; and making flexible career plans that allow for a family life. The author is a journalist and financial specialist at *Newsday.*

77   Jaffe, Natalie. "Men's Jobs for Women: Toward Occupational Equality." Public Affairs Pamphlet no. 606. Washington, D.C.: Public Affairs Committee, 1982.

A brief introduction to the trends and issues for women in nontraditional jobs.

78   Kahn, William A., and Crosby, Faye. "Discriminating between Attitudes and Discriminatory Behaviors: Change and Stasis." In *Women and Work: An Annual Review,* vol. 1, edited by Laurie Larwood, Ann H. Stromberg, and Barbara A. Gutek. Beverly Hills, Calif.: Sage Publications, 1985.

This article points out that discrimination and antifemale prejudice have been factors in the American workplace, probably since the early days of the country's history. The authors search for an answer to a central question: "Why, when many people now have more egalitarian views, does discrimination remain so pervasive?" The authors discuss the findings of recent surveys that document attitudes toward working women. The studies indicate significant attitude changes regarding women's participation, equal pay, discrimination, and day care. But, in contrast, the authors point out that behavior in the workplace has not changed as much. They find convincing evidence of persistent sex discrimination that manifests itself in nonemployment, segregation, unequal compensation, and sexual harassment. Their explanation for this state of affairs contains several basic points. (1) Attitudes reported in surveys may document people's desire to answer in a socially desirable way. (2) Surveys ask questions in vague ways and are unreliable; for instance, questions often do not ask about specific ways of treating women in the workplace. (3) The samples don't test views of decision makers whose actions determine women's employment status. (4) There are many complex attitudes toward women that aren't surveyed, and these attitudes compete with each other. The authors discuss the context in which changing attitudes and static behavior exist in institutions. They emphasize the way organizations reinforce discriminatory behaviors, suggesting that in some ways organizations reflect the larger culture. They point out that individuals behave as a function of their location in organization structure. They quote Rosabeth Moss Kanter's work and say "discriminatory practices are more often than not responses by individuals to system pressure, particularly those connected with the uncertainties" of legitimacy, evaluation, communication, and loyalty. Also, these behaviors are often unintentional rather than deliberate.

The authors suggest ways people can speed equal treatment of women and put three models forward. The first model suggests that attitudes are changing and that behavior will follow once the realization of injustice occurs. The second model says that systemic change is partly a function of individuals' experiences and changes. Also, as individuals come to terms with their anxiety in systems, then groups will come to terms with group anxieties such as those characterizing class struggles, and social systems will change. The third model assumes modification of institutional structures. Organizations must devise and execute policies explicitly designed to empower women and enhance their opportunities. The authors point out in closing that individuals create structural, institutional, and societal change. This change necessitates political behavior in a variety of individual situations. Working women can complain, compare, and question. The authors conclude that "recognizing and pointing out organizational practices that have the potential to discriminate against women is the way in which women alert both one another and the men in their systems of the paradox of expressed egalitarianism and behavioral discrimination." This research is recommended to all readers.

79 Kanter, Rosabeth Moss. *Men and Women of the Corporation.* New York: Basic Books, 1977.

Cited again and again in this literature. Especially valuable are the insights about tokenism and the impact of organizational structure on women's ability to advance.

80 Kanter, Rosabeth Moss, and Stein, Barry. "The Gender Pioneers: Women in the Industrial Sales Force." In *Life in Organizations: Workplaces as People Experience Them.* New York: Basic Books, 1979.

Kanter and Stein look at one group of women on an occupational frontier.

81 Katsekas, B. S. "The Effects of Progressive Relaxation and Guided Fantasy on the Reduction of Career Anxiety in Undergraduate Women Exploring Nontraditional Careers." Ed.D. dissertation, University of Maine, 1979.

82 Keller, Evelyn Fox. "Women and Basic Research: Respecting the Unexpected." *Technology Review,* November-December 1984, pp. 44-47.

A significant part of this article focuses on the work of cytogeneticist Barbara McClintock, winner of the 1983 Nobel Prize in physiology and medicine, who possessed a determination "to claim science as a human rather than a male endeavor." Her worldview gives special attention to difference and idiosyncrasy and assigns particular value to intrinsic difference. Fox Keller asks: What would happen if men and women and science developed in a world free of stereotypes suggesting that the world of science is a rational, masculine world? She asks: "How might science be different if contructed in a gender-free environment while still being recognizable as something we would all agree to call science?"

83 Kleiman, Carol. "Tokens of Respect: What Is It Like to Work in a Heavily Male Field?" *Chicago Tribune,* 25 January 1987, sec. 6, p. 5.

Interviews with four women in nontraditional fields: a chief executive officer of her own contracting firm (who is also black); a Hispanic woman who is a detective; a product project scheduler and material control analyst; and a senior claims representative for fire and casualty insurance claims.

84 Kleiman, Carol. "U.S. Women Forgo Political Envelope Stuffing for Areas with Clout and Pay." *Chicago Tribune.*
    Mentions a survey report, released by the Center for the American Woman and Politics at Rutgers University, which finds that governors are naming more women than ever to state cabinets. The report says that 17.9 of these posts nationwide are held by women. (Examined at Midwest Women's Center Library, Chicago.)

85 Klemesrud, Judy. "Women Hammer Away at Male Job Bastions." *New York Times,* 22 November 1972, p. C42.
    The article begins, "They still cannot be fathers or Canadian Mounties. But many of the other all male bastions have come tumbling down in recent months as women have been hired for jobs that were once reserved for the hairy arms of men." Klemesrud proceeds to give us a gold mine of first women, one of whom is "Michigan's first female exterminator for Aardvark of Detroit. (They are billing her as the 'prettiest female exterminator since Lucretia Borgia.')" She also profiles Margaret Decker, "believed to be the first woman licensed to be a dynamite blaster in the state of Pennsylvania." A fascinating summary of breakthrough women in nontraditional jobs at the time.

86 LaBastille, Anne, ed. *Women and Wilderness.* San Francisco: Sierra Club Books, 1980.
    Includes a very useful bibliography.

87 LaFontaine, Edward, and Ledeau, Leslie. "The Frequency, Sources, and Correlates of Sexual Harrassment among Women in Traditional Male Occupations." *Sex Roles: A Journal of Research* 15, no. 7-8 (October 1986): 433-42.

88 Laws, Judith Long. *The Second X: Sex Role and Social Role.* New York: Elsevier, 1979.
    Laws divides her book into six sections: An introduction raising issues in the study of sex roles; "Woman as Worker"; "Woman as Housewife"; "Woman as Object"; "Woman as Girl-Child"; "Woman as Androgyne." She says "the aim of this book is to trace the systematic consequences of being born female – that is, bearing the second X on the genetic code." Laws points out that "although the sex labeling of

jobs can contribute to the scarcity of women and men in sex-atypical jobs, the operation of prejudice and discrimination against the few can add to this problem. The highly visible token woman may provide a role model for aspiring women, but if they observe that she is harassed, discriminated against, and miserable, they are unlikely to follow in her footsteps."

89   Lembright, Murial Faltz, and Riemer, Jeffrey W. "Women Truckers' Problems and the Impact of Sponsorship." *Work and Occupations* 9, no. 4 (November 1982): 457-74.

This sociological article includes the following sections: methods; social characteristics of women truckers; and women truckers' problems (physical obstacles, health problems, and socially based tensions and troubles.) The authors surveyed ninety women truckers via an open-ended questionnaire in 1979, and their responses represent the core data of this article. The findings are particularly informative regarding the specific kinds of sexual discrimination the women experience, and the authors discuss at length the impact of sponsorship on the success of the women truckers. The authors point out that up to this time women truckers have largely been overlooked by social science researchers. They assert that "the media representatives and others in a journalistic rendition, have provided an image, albeit distorted, of the long-haul woman trucker." This is a valuable and important piece of research. A significant four-page bibliography is appended. (Examined as preprint paper at Business and Professional Women's Foundation Library, Washington, D.C.)

90   Lemkau, Jeanne Parr. "Personality and Background Characteristics of Women in Male-Dominated Occupations: A Review." *Psychology of Women Quarterly* 4, no. 2 (Winter 1979): 221-40.

The author discusses particularly the psychological research literature published from 1930 through 1976 on women in professional occupations where men predominate. She draws many interesting conclusions from these research reports, including that personality data show such women to have many competency traits related to the masculine stereotype and ideal. She concludes from the literature that women in nontraditional occupations are emotionally healthy and have good coping skills, although they may experience situational stress. She mentions that the women share many background characteristics that foster achievement. These characteristics include having parents with high levels of education, being of recently foreign ancestry, first-born status, high family stability, parental encouragement of androgynous exploration, high maternal employment, and strong paternal support for both mother and daughter. Lemkau concludes her article with a recommendation that four research initiatives take place in future studies. She calls for research comparing women employed in the trades with women employed in traditional jobs where academic achievement is not important to allow a clear separation of the personality and background characteristics and nontraditional career choice. She calls for direct comparisons of women and men in nontraditional and traditional occupations. She thinks research should answer the question, "How do the different cultural stereotypes interact with personality and background to influence career choice?" She also thinks more refined assessments are needed of contributions of situational factors, personality, and background to influence atypical career choice. Finally, she calls for study of determinants of competent functions among women in any occupational sphere. She wants to dispel myths about women at work by studies determining female excellence and the personality and background correlates of it.

This article is based on the author's 1977 Ph.D. dissertation at the University of Rhode Island.

91   Lewis, V., and Kaltrieder, L. W. *Attempts to Overcome Stereotyping in Vocational Education.* University Park, Pa.: Institute for Research on Human Resources, 1976.

Found that girls in nontraditional vocational training courses name male peers as their most frequent critics.

92   Louisiana Bureau for Women. *Forty-Six Pioneers: Louisiana Women in Non-Traditional Jobs.* Baton Rouge: Office of Human Services, Louisiana Department of Health and Human Resources. Office of Human Services, November 1977, 48 pp.

A research project (published in ring binders) telling results of statewide training project and giving biographies of talented women who succeeded.

93   McClure Lundberg Associates. *Young Women in Non-Traditional Occupations Technical Assistance Guide.* Washington, D.C.: McClure Lundberg Associates, 1978.

94 McClure Lundberg Associates. *Young Women in Non-Traditional Occupations: Why and How? A Systematic Approach for Job Development.* Washington, D.C.: McClure Lundberg Associates, 1979.

Workbook to accompany association's technical assistance guide (see above). Available from McClure Lundberg Associates, Suite LL-1, 1717 Massachusetts Ave. NW, Washington, DC 20036.

95 McIlwee, Judith S. "Work Satisfaction among Women in Non-Traditional Occupations." *Work and Occupations* 9 (1982): 299-335.

McIlwee was an assistant professor of sociology at Salem College in North Carolina at the time of this research. She worked with data gathered under a grant awarded by the National Institute of Mental Health to Mary Walshok, author of *Blue-Collar Women: Pioneers on a Male Frontier* (see entries 128 and 197).

The research describes sources of work satisfaction and dissatisfaction among a sample of 86 California women entering male-dominated skilled and semiskilled occupations in 1975. The findings suggest that movement of women into these jobs, while being a positive step toward reducing inequality in the work force, will not eliminate problems for the women involved with actually achieving satisfaction.

96 Meyer, Herbert H., and Lee, Mary Dean. *The Integration of Females into Traditionally Male-Oriented Jobs: Experiences of Certain Public Utility Companies.* A report prepared for the Employment and Training Administration. U.S. Department of Labor. Washington, D.C.: U.S. Government Printing Office, 1976.

The authors found "that because many women felt the need to prove themselves and be accepted by men, they had to do more work than would have been required of a man."

97 Michelson, Maureen. *Women and Work: Photographs and Personal Writings.* Pasadena, Calif.: New Sage Press, 1986.

Photographs of and essays by eighty-five women at work are included. Nontraditional jobs mentioned in this book include orchestra conductor, coal miner, fire fighter, pilot, farmer, cattle rancher, psychiatric chaplain, stationary engineer, welder, farrier, cabinetmaker, jockey, pastor, and architect.

Photographs compiled by Michael R. Dressler and Maureen R. Michelson. A beautiful book and a good way to hear the voices of the women themselves. Their strength, determination, and perseverance are evident on every page.

98   Milvid, Beth. "Breaking In: Experience in the Male-Dominated Professions." *Women and Therapy* 2 (Fall 1983): 67-79.

An important article, giving revealing insights into the psychological issues shared by some women in nontraditional professions. Milvid is a clinical psychologist in San Francisco, and this article is based on research with thirty middle-class white women in nontraditional professions in the Bay Area. Ten were bankers, ten were lawyers, and ten were architects. None of the women in the study had practiced her profession for more than five years. They shared many experiences across their professions: they had not expected the start-up period to be so grueling; trying to be feminist and do the work raised many questions and challenges for them; and most of the women felt compelled to mask certain aspects of their identities as they integrated their workplaces. Milvid found that all of the women "underwent a discrete process of emotional development." She concluded: (1) Work provided a high level of personal and professional satisfaction. (2) Entering a male-dominated profession involved a process of change and development. (3) The first couple of years at work were the most psychologically strenuous. (4) Few women expected any difficulties with being accepted by coworkers in their chosen field. (5) Most experienced a strong sense of visibility and heightened self-consciousness. (6) Subjects believed they were not taken seriously until they had proven their competence. (7) Work took all their time and energy, and the women felt that "an ease and impromptu quality had vanished from their lives." (8) Becoming more assertive was valued but created inner conflict. (9) The women were starting to question the central role of work within their lives. They were beginning to fantasize about more flexible and collaborative organizations. In perhaps one of Milvid's most important statements, she says the work environment for these women can be filled with great ambiguity and anxiety, but "to date most of that anxiety has been publicly denied." She closes her article by discussing some implications that she sees for clinical practice. She makes some sensitive observations about the "rigid and defensive styles some women in nontraditional fields adopt in order to survive," and she suggests that clinicians attribute these to sex discrimination and bias within our culture so that they can work together with women in an effective and dynamic fashion.

99 "Nation Cries for Women." *Washington Post,* 1 March 1966.

An editorial in the "For and about Women" section in the *Washington Post* discussing a recent speech by President Lyndon Johnson. He announced a study group on careers for women. He felt the nation needed such a study because a worker shortage had been predicted for the future. He announced that the needs of the nation could not be met unless more women were trained to enter the professional work force.

100 Newland, Kathleen. *Women, Men, and the Division of Labor.* Worldwatch Paper no. 37. Washington, D.C.: Worldwatch Institute, May 1980, 43 pp.

Newland's presentation of global information is divided into the following sections: "What the GNP Leaves Out"; "Paid Labor: A Man's World No Longer"; "Unpaid Labor: Women's Work Still"; "The Division of Labor between Women and Men"; and "The Symmetrical Family."

101 Nieva, Veronica F. "Work and Family Linkages." In *Women and Work: An Annual Review,* vol. 1, edited by Laurie Larwood, Ann H. Stromberg, and Barbara A. Gutek. Beverly Hills, Calif.: Sage Publications, 1985.

Nieva chronicles recent changes in the structures in American society and suggests these changes have eroded the traditional separation between the worlds of work and family. She provides a research overview of the impact of work on family, the impact of family on work, and the individual and institutional mechanisms for handling work and family interdependencies.

102 Nieva, Veronica F., and Gutek, Barbara A. *Women and Work: A Psychological Perspective.* New York: Praeger, 1981.

The authors discuss the context of women's work, their career choices, the factors affecting their decision to work, the combination of work and family, their integration into the workplace, their performance evaluation, their leadership and achievements, their organizational rewards, and approaches to change. The sections on "Career Pioneers," "Integrating Women into the Workplace," and "Rewards" are highly relevant to this study because the authors provide excellent research literature analysis.

103   Patterson, Michelle, and Engelberg, Laurie. "Women in Male-Dominated Professions." In *Women Working,* edited by Ann H. Stromberg and Shirley Harkness. Palo Alto, Calif.: Mayfield, 1978.

An early discussion of the difficulty token women have in supporting other women.

104   Porter, Jeanne Harber, ed. *Nontraditional Resources Catalog.* Fort Wayne: Fort Wayne Women's Bureau, 49 pp.

Designed to provide a listing of materials relevant to nontraditional careers, including work-pattern information on flex time, job sharing, and industry-supported child care. Cites articles, facts on women workers, films, publications, test preparations, slides, cassettes, and wall charts, and gives some tips for women searching for a job in construction.

105   Prial, Frank J. "More Women Work at Traditional Male Jobs." *New York Times,* 15 November 1982, pp. 1, C20.

About the fields younger women have made inroads into, including those of bartenders, bakers, pharmacists, scientists, lawyers, and judges.

106   Project NEW. *Women's Work: Skilled Trades.* Bloomington, Ind.: Project NEW, c. 1978, 35 pp.

A brochure describing some new job alternatives, available from: Helene Pizzini, Director, Human Resources Department, Project NEW, Box 100, Bloomington, IN 47402.

107   Roby, Pamela. *Women in the Workplace: Proposals for Research and Policy Concerning the Conditions of Women in Industrial and Service Jobs.* Cambridge, Mass.: Schenkman Publishers, 1981.

In the first chapter of this monograph, Roby states: "Before entering nontraditional jobs, women should first become familiar with problems that may be encountered, how to cope with those problems, and how to form better relationships with their supervisors. A book containing this information could usefully be published and accompanied by training and consciousness-raising conferences for women. Forepersons, union stewards, and workers in traditionally male areas could be given human relations sensitivity training to prepare them for women working in their traditionally all-male divisions or shops. Men and women in traditionally all-male departments might also be brought together in joint problem-solving meetings held during working hours. These in-service training or consciousness-raising sessions should include efforts to discover and deal with men's fears about women entering traditionally male jobs. The many men – young and old, black and white – who willingly assist women in learning traditionally male jobs might be involved in leading these sessions. Stewards, supervisors, and workers who actively assist women in breaking into new jobs should be rewarded with bonuses just as they would if they performed some other aspect of their job especially well."

Later in the work, after summarizing past and current research, the author states that basic changes are needed in the economy before living conditions of blue-collar women are greatly improved. She states her criteria for determining research priorities: (1) the number of women whose living conditions could be improved by the proposed research or policy change; (2) the degree of improvement of women's living conditions; (3) the relative need of the population; (4) the implementation of the improvements in the most efficient and feasible manner; (5) the researchers' connections with relevant change agents; (6) the complexity of the proposed research; (7) the extent to which the research process could raise the consciousness of the target population in regard to their economic and social needs; (8) the type of broad societal changes required to meet those needs. This book contains a wealth of analytical information and is highly recommended.

108   Safran, Claire. "What Men Do to Women on the Job." *Redbook*, November 1976, pp. 149, 217-224.

About the high incidence of experience with harassment in a national sample of working women.

109   Schroedel, Jean Reith. *Alone in a Crowd*. Philadelphia: Temple University Press, 1985.

Schroedel organizes her book into the following sections: feminism; occupational safety and health; race; unions; and family. Into these sections, she places the results of twenty-four interviews with women working in many of the blue-collar trades. She includes a steel hauler, a pipe fitter, a fire fighter, a carpenter, and a shipwright, to name the first five. What emerges are many profiles of complex and different women, both heterosexual and lesbian, who are struggling to make a success of sexual integration in their workplaces. Through her oral histories, insight into the contemporary work realities for these women emerge.

110 Shuchat, Jo, Guinier, Genii, and Douglas, Aileen. *The Nuts and Bolts of NTO: A Handbook for Recruitment, Training, Support Services, and Placement of Women in Non-Traditional Occupations.* Cambridge, Mass.: The Women's Outreach Project, Technical Education Research Centers, 1981.

Jo Shuchat is the director of the Sex Equity in Education program at Women's Action Alliance and has created an excellent handbook for recruitment, training, support services and placement of women in nontraditional occupations. It is addressed to directors, placement specialists, trainers, teachers, administrators, guidance and career counselors, job-training programs in the public sector and private industry, women's centers and programs, and specialists in public policy and women's studies. Organized into eight important chapters covering planning and evaluation, coordinating resources, outreach, career exploration, support services (obstacles at home, work, school), and placement, she concludes with ten strong appendixes, including an excellent bibliography and media list. The handbook is the best of its kind examined during this study. (Note: The second edition of this book, listed under "Jo Shuchat Sanders" and published in 1986 by Scarecrow Press, was significantly expanded. It features annotated listings of the most important organizations and state and national agencies, the best and most recent print and audiovisual resources, recent legislation that effects nontraditional occupations for women, and the funding opportunities of the Carl D. Perkins Vocational Education Act.

111 Stockard, Jean. *Sex Equity in Educational Leadership [SEEL]: An Analysis of a Planned Social Change Project.* Newton, Mass.: Women's Educational Equity Act (WEEA) Publishing Center, 1982.

The volume reviews the original plans and goals of the SEEL Project, discusses what happened in the attempts to implement these plans, examines why the results have occurred, and presents tentative suggestions for others wanting to attain equity in educational administration. It was sponsored by the University of Oregon Center for Educational Policy and Management, and it is available from the WEEA Publishing Center, 55 Chapel Street, Newton, MA 02160.

112 Swatko, Mary K. "What's in a Title? Personality, Job Aspirations, and the Nontraditional Woman." *Journal of Vocational Behavior* 18, no. 2 (April 1981): 174-83.

In a study of bank tellers and their use of the title "Ms.," Swatko found that self-designation of "Ms." indicates a greater tendency to be a role innovator aspiring to future occupations with a greater percentage of men.

113 Tangri, Sandra Schwartz. "Role Innovation in Occupational Choice." Ph.D. dissertation, University of Michigan, 1969.

Cited in Ann Kathleen Burlew's article (*Psychology of Women Quarterly* 6, no. 3 [Spring 1982]: 12-26) on black females' experiences in nontraditional professions. Report on this doctoral research later published in the *Journal of Social Issues* 28, no. 2 (1972): 177-99.

114 Taylor, Beth. "Been Down So Long." *Friends Journal,* 15 March 1980, pp. 15-19.

About a project carried out in two counties in West Virginia to prepare rural women to enter nontraditional jobs. It was part of the Appalachian Women's Advocacy Project (which also operated in Virginia and Kentucky). New Employment for Women was sponsored by the American Friends Service Committee and financed in part by the U.S. Department of Labor, Women's Bureau. (Lincoln County, West Virginia, was one of the counties where the project was carried out.)

115 "Teens Look to Nontraditional Careers." *Christian Science Monitor,* 9 December 1981.

An article about a study of eighth- and tenth-grade students conducted by the Institute of Occupational Education at Cornell University that found that students cite their parents as influential in their career choices and that they are slowly preparing themselves for nontraditional careers in larger numbers. Helen C. Veres, an educational researcher with the institute in the Department of Education at Cornell, surveyed 460 students in New York State and also gathered information from 127 parents.

116   Terbony, J.R., and Ilgan, D. R. "A Theoretical Approach to Sex Discrimination in Traditionally Masculine Occupations." *Organizational Behavior and Human Performance* 13 (1975): 352-76.

The authors explore both access and treatment discrimination as well as the profound implications of equality theory for women in nontraditional fields. They clearly explain the possibility that, if women are seen as performing under involuntary constraints in nontraditional fields, then they should "be attributed greater inputs and accordingly greater rewards." The authors constructed an in-basket exercise as an experimental simulation of administrative decision-making skills by men and women engineers. Results of the exercise are discussed. In addition to raising many provocative ideas, the authors provide a strong supporting bibliography of relevant research primarily published in the 1960s and early 1970s.

117   Trigg, L. J., and Perlman, D. "Social Influences on Women's Pursuits of a Nontraditional Career." *Psychology of Women Quarterly* 1 (1976): 138-50.

Trigg and Perlman's findings do not agree with Tangri's and must be compared. They found in their sample that women entering nontraditional careers had lower affiliative needs, considered being married and having children less important, and enjoyed support from significant others. They collected data from 153 nursing students and 78 medical students and dental students.

118   U.S. Department of Labor. Women's Bureau. "Are Women Taking Men's Jobs?" (rev.) In *Labor D.C.,* Ser. WB-63, no. 448. Washington, D.C.: U.S. Government Printing Office, June 1963, 2 pp.

An introduction to the fears of the time.

119   U.S. Department of Labor. Women's Bureau. *Non-Traditional Jobs for Women.* Regional Manpower Training Institute, Region III Department of Labor, 9-11 December 1975, 100 pp.

Training materials for a conference, including institute handouts published in Pennsylvania, West Virginia, Maryland, Delaware, D.C., and Virginia, all stapled together. Conference attendees learned training techniques, including how to teach women to recognize and deal with discrimination. Very useful. Examined at U.S. Department of Labor Women's Bureau, Midwest Region, Chicago.

120 U.S. Department of Labor. Women's Bureau. *Women in Nontraditional Employment: A Selected List of Publications, Slides, and Films.* Washington, D.C.: U.S. Government Printing Office. 1978.

121 U.S. Department of Labor. Women's Bureau. *Women in Nontraditional Jobs: A Program Model.* Boston: Nontraditional Occupations Program for Women, 1978, 79 pp.

The Women's Bureau was pushing at this time for the integration of women into nontraditional jobs especially in the building trades. This publication and the one listed in the next entry describes the development of training programs to prepare women for new forms of employment.

122 U.S. Department of Labor. Women's Bureau. *Women in Nontraditional Jobs: A Program Model.* Denver: Better Jobs for Women, 1978, 60 pp.

123 U.S. Department of Labor. Women's Bureau. *Women in Nontraditional Jobs: A Workshop Mode; Working with Employers to Develop Jobs.* Washington, D.C.: U.S. Government Printing Office, 1978, 20 pp.

124 U.S. Department of Labor. Women's Bureau. Coal Employment Project (CEP). *How Women Can Make Breakthroughs into Nontraditional Industries.* Washington, D.C.: U.S. Government Printing Office, 1985, 50 pp.

Opening statement by Leonore Cole-Alexander, director of the Women's Bureau, saying that the Women's Bureau has program guides so others can duplicate efforts shown promising in pilot projects. Then an introduction to CEP and its efforts follows. This is a mysterious publication as no mention is made of who wrote it, or who founded the CEP, or whether the Women's Bureau ever supported them.

125   Vitters, Major Alan G. *Report of the Admission of Women to the U.S. Military Academy (Project Athena II).* United States Military Academy at West Point, Department of Behavioral Sciences and Leadership, West Point, N.Y.: June 1978, 89 pp.

A comprehensive, systematic update o the analysis of coeducation at the U.S. Military Academy at West Point from June 1977 to April 1978. The researchers inquired into the following aspects of coeducation: characteristics of entering classes; academic, physical, and military training performance; resignation rates over time; the assignment of women to the staff and faculty; and approaches toward educational awareness on the issue.

126   Waite, Linda J., and Berryman, Sue E. *Women in Non-Traditional Occupations, Choice and Turnover.* Santa Monica, Calif.: the Rand Corporation, 1985.

Research on work absence is discussed. Preliminary findings of research on women in nontraditional civilian and military sectors.

127   Wall, James A., and Vertue, Robert. "Women as Negotiators." *Business Horizons* 19 (April 1976):2.

Brief article describing women's potential contributions to conflict resolution and their absence from the field in the past.

128   Walshok, Mary Lindenstein. *Blue-Collar Women: Pioneers on a Male Frontier.* New York: Doubleday, Anchor Press, 1981.

An insightful and respectful introduction to the characteristics and motivations of women in nontraditional blue-collar work. Walshok was a pioneer herself; this is probably the first book-length study of blue-collar women in nontraditional fields. A landmark study. (For more detailed annotation, see entry 197.)

129   Wardle, Miriam G. "Women's Physiological Reactions to Physically Demanding Work." *Psychology of Women Quarterly,* Winter 1976, pp. 151-59.

130   Wertheimer, Barbara M., and Nelson, Ann H., eds. *Women as Third-Party Neutrals: Gaining Acceptability.* Ithaca, N.Y.: Cornell

University, New York State School of Industrial and Labor Relations, 1978.

These are the proceedings from a conference sponsored by the Institute for Education and Research on Women and Work, New York State School of Industrial and Labor Relations, Cornell University, and the American Arbitration Association, held 12 February 1977, New York, N.Y. The idea at the time was to discuss the low proportion of women representatives in careers as third-party neutrals: that is, fact finders, mediators, conciliators, and arbitrators. History of women's involvement in the field since World War II included. Contains a useful glossary of labor arbitration terms.

131 Wetherby, Terry. *Conversations: Working Women Talk about Doing a "Man's Job."* Millbrae, Calif.: Les Femmes Press, 1977.

Wetherby, a writer, became a welder at the Triple A Shipyard in San Francisco to earn good money and allow her the freedom to work on her writing. She says, "This book is about rugged individualism and self-determination." It consists of twenty-two interviews, chosen from over thirty conducted by Wetherby, and it provides information about the existence and absence of discrimination and about discouragement and encouragement in unlikely places. The common denominators among these women are a strong self-image, hard work, and a culture that casts them as oddities. The book includes interviews with women who work in the following jobs: butcher, grain-elevator manager, karate-school director, television vice president, welder, truck driver, carpenter, stuntwoman, mill supervisor, chief of police, commercial pilot, dairy officer, director of a handyperson's enterprise, electronics mechanic, law-school dean, chaplain, race-car driver, biochemist, pesticide inspector, bank president, naturopathic physician, and chairperson of the board of a business firm.

132 "What's a Nice Girl Like You Doing in a Place Like This?" *Ebony,* June 1977, 103-4.

Includes an interview with a security guard, attorney's investigator, construction worker, pipe fitter, bus driver, hot-press operator, and sales representative. Photos of women on the job are included.

133   Wilkinson, Carroll Wetzel. "Women in Nontraditional Fields and Feminism: An Uneasy Connection?" *West Virginia Law Review* 91, no. 1 (Fall 1988-89): 153-64.

Wilkinson speculates about some of the reasons women in nontraditional fields may feel uncomfortable about the women's movement, and why some feminists cannot accept the actions of female pioneers in their workplaces. She discusses the wide spectrum of values regarding gender consciousness, the wide gaps in understanding and perspective that exist between the two groups, the overall difficulty caused by labeling and stereotyping in the first place, the divisions caused by class consciousness, and the phenomenon of "the closet feminist syndrome" in which women believe in feminist principles but experience discomfort when confronted with the demands of activism. Overall, she puts forth a hope that these gaps in understanding between women can close and that the community of women will be strengthened by mutual tolerance and respect. She points out that researchers have confirmed what common sense might tell us anyway: that positive attitudes toward other women may increase women's own sense of self-value.

134   Wilkinson, Carroll Wetzel. "Work: Challenges to Occupational Segregation." In *The Women's Annual,* no. 5, edited by Mary Drake McFeely. Boston: G. K. Hall & Co., 1985.

The chapter introduces critical issues for women who have chosen to pioneer on male occupational frontiers, and it profiles, as of 1985, the latest published information on the subject.

135   *Womanpower: A Special Issue of Manpower Magazine,* November 1975, 44 pp.

Every article important, especially "In the Manner of Rosie the Riveter" by Edwin Harris and "How to Succeed in a Journeyman's World" by B. Kimball Baker.

136   Women Employed Institute. "Increasing Women's Access to Non-Traditional Jobs." A discussion paper prepared for the Women Employed Institute's Collaborative Conference, 5 February 1987. Chicago, Ill.: Women Employed Institute, 1987, 14 pp.

Based on statistical and survey research on the vocational education and training programs offered by the Chicago public schools, the city colleges, and the Mayor's Office of Employment and Training.

The research focused on why the majority of females do not participate in these programs that would prepare them to enter male-dominated jobs. General findings revealed that: (1) exploration of career opportunities for young girls is often limited by stereotypical views and/or lack of knowledge of counselors, teachers, and the girls themselves; (2) selection of and entry into appropriate educational and training programs are hampered by inadequate counseling, little or no outreach and recruitment by institutions and training programs, and often outright discriminatory practices; (3) female participation in nontraditional programs is sometimes met with hostility from colleagues and teachers, and little or no peer support is available; (4) actual job placement and retention may be difficult due to union and employer attitudes.

137 "Women Make Headway in Nontraditional Careers." *National Business Woman,* August-September 1988, pp. 18-23.

Includes discussion of new statistics from the U.S. Bureau of Labor Statistics on selected occupations by gender and profiles of several women in male-intensive jobs.

138 "Women Said Gaining in Male-Dominated Fields." *Chronicle of Higher Education,* 19 June 1978, p. 2.

Points out that women are now carrying a larger share of college degrees awarded in traditionally male-dominated fields. Between 1971 and 1976 the number of B.A. degrees earned by women increased in all but five of the twenty-four academic disciplines examined by the National Center for Education Statistics. Business and management rose from 9 percent to 20 percent; law, from 5 percent to 19 percent; and agriculture and natural resources, from 4 percent to 18 percent.

139 Yanico, B. J., Hardin, S.F., and McLaughlin, K. B. "Androgyny and Traditional vs. Nontraditional Major Choice among College Freshmen." *Journal of Vocational Behavior* 12 (1987): 261-69.

As a group, women who had chosen engineering as a major scored a higher androgynous rating than did men in engineering or women in the traditional field of home economics. Yanico and colleagues were interested to find out more about a possible relationship between androgyny and career choice. One of the hypotheses they tested was: Feminine-typed women in engineering would show less satisfaction and certainty in their choice of major than androgynous or masculine-typed women. They found that feminine-typed women were significantly less satisfied and tended to be less certain of their choice of a career field.

140   Zelman, Patricia G. *Women, Work, and National Policy: The Kennedy-Johnson Years.* Ann Arbor, Mich.: University Microfilms International Research Press, 1980.

Chronicles history of the linkage of sex and race discrimination in federal policies and legislation. Excellent bibliography, with primary sources. Based on her 1980 Ph.D. dissertation at Ohio State University, "Development of Equal Opportunity for Women as a National Policy, 1960-1967."

Women at Work in Selected Nontraditional Fields

Trades

I didn't start thinking about nontraditional work until I heard the carpenters were looking for women. But as soon as the possibility was mentioned, my imagination went with it. I liked the idea of working with wood. There's a lot of independence in a trade. You work from job to job, not necessarily full-time. Of course the money is excellent.

– Elaine Carfield
Quoted in *Alone in a Crowd*, 1985, by Jean Reith Schroedel

In May 1989, with the introduction of federal legislation supporting the expansion of nontraditional work training for women (Senate bill no. 975), societal recognition of the need to open more work opportunities to women reached a new stage. Senators Hatch, Metzenbaum, Kasselbaum, Pell, and Kennedy cosponsored the bill entitled the Nontraditional Employment for Women Act. Advocates for women helped shape the legislation, and even if the bill does not become law, the writing of it is evidence, as is the literature in this section, that an exciting but very difficult struggle for women is being waged in the blue-collar employment sector. The literature reveals that many of the same social dynamics that receive so much attention in the professions also prevail for women doing blue-collar work.

Apprenticeship and Nontraditional Employment for Women

141   ANEW. *Renovations: Changing Your Shape for New Forms of Work.*
Renton, Wash.: ANEW, 1982.
A guide to the physical demands of selected jobs and specific
strength-building exercises for women to prepare their bodies to meet
those demands. ANEW is a nonprofit agency that orients, counsels,
trains, and places women in apprenticeship programs and other blue-
collar jobs. Classroom training covers trades math, blueprint reading,
safety and building-trades terminology, use and care of hand and power
tools. Lab projects include threading pipe, mixing and pouring concrete,
erecting and climbing scaffolding, tying steel, arc welding, and
oxyacetylene cutting. "Labor and management representatives who
designed the course agreed that no matter how many technical skills
students acquired, they would still be unable to compete in the trades
unless they increased their physical strength and endurance." Sections:
physical demands of the trades, strength building for the trades, starting
your fitness program, sample fire fighters' test. Renton Vocational
Technical Institute thanked in acknowledgments.

142   "Breaking Job Barriers: A Personal Interview Report on Women
Invading Men's Fields." *Parents Magazine,* April 1978, pp. 56-57.
An interesting series of interviews with women who work as
welders, college presidents, auto mechanics, and airport supervisors.
Emphasis is placed on their sense that their work is not having negative
effects on their children.

143   Briggs, Norma. *Women in Apprenticeship–Why Not?* Manpower
Research Monograph no. 33. Washington, D.C.: U.S. Department of
Labor, Manpower Administration,   1974, 34 pp.
Based on insights gained in three years of collaborative effort
in the Women in Wisconsin Apprenticeships program.

144   Cleveland Concentrated Employment Program and Institute of Arts
Studies. *Women in Blue-Collar Jobs: A Report on Women and
Industries in Cleveland, Ohio.* Cleveland, Ohio: 1974.
Sections in book include: review of literature; empirical
research into women and industries in Cleveland; conclusions and
recommendations.

145 "Coalition Cites Extensive Sex and Race Discrimination." *Chicago Defender,* 17 December 1985.

About data released by the Southeast Women's Employment Coalition regarding race and sex discrimination in the federally funded road and highway construction projects.

146 Cook, Alice H., et al. *Women and Trade Unions in Eleven Industrialized Countries.* Philadelphia: Temple University Press, 1984.

147 Crittenden, Ann. "Study Finds Women Lagging in Craft Jobs." *New York Times,* 26 February 1979, sec. D, p. 3.

A report by the Conference Board has been published that shows women are slowly winning more high-paying white-collar jobs, but it also shows that they have made virtually no progress in the male-dominated areas in industry.

148 Davis, H. C. "The Impact of Orientation to Entry-Level Coal-Mining Occupations upon the Self-Concept of Women Seeking Training for Entry-Level Coal-Mining Occupations." Ph.D. dissertation, Ohio State University, 1980.

149 Deaux, Kay, and Ullman, Joseph C. *Women of Steel: Female Blue-Collar Workers in the Basic Steel Industry.* New York: Praeger, 1983.

An excellent study.

150 Dennis, E. M. "Women in Selected Male-Dominated Trades: Their Perceptions of Social Workers and Clerical Workers." Ed.D. dissertation, University of Cincinnati, 1981.

151 Eastes, Meg, ed. *Opening Trade Barriers: Final Report.* Fort Wayne: Fort Wayne Women's Bureau, 1979.

152   Egan, Christine. "Apprenticeship Now." *Occupational Outlook Quarterly* 22 (Summer 1978): 2-19.
An overview of apprenticeship programs.

153   Foreman, Judy. "Making the Grade in the Trades." *Boston Globe,* 7 October 1978, p. 7.
About a union-backed skilled-trades training program for women called the Women in Construction Project in Brighton, Northhampton, and Plymouth, Massachusetts. The article contains statistics on how women, blacks, and other minorities rank in the total number of workers nationally in the construction trades.

154   Friedman, Jane. "Women: New Facet of the Diamond Trade." *New York Times Spotlight Sunday,* 18 February 1979, p. 2.
Lengthy article about women in the diamond trade, working as cutters and jewelers. An interesting profile of an unusual field for a woman.

155   Garvin, Mary G. *Blue-Collar Jobs for Women: A Guide for Trainers and Managers.* New York: M. G. Garvin, 1981.
A practical manual, arranged in units that include an overview of women and work, a section on supportive services, and information on job development.

156   Goldstein, Rikki, ed. *Opening Trade Barriers: Sex-Role Awareness Tools.* Fort Wayne: Fort Wayne Women's Bureau, 1979, 15 pp.
A brief introduction to the constraints of unquestioned sex roles.

157   Grossman, Ron. "Choices: Goal for Blue-Collar Women." *Chicago Tribune,* 21 November 1985.
This article discusses the formation of Southwest Women Working Together, a neighborhood-based social-service agency founded, staffed, and maintained by working-class women. Members do not identify with *Ms.* readers. They feel they are confronting the stiff realities of a traditionalist community. Nevertheless, they are conducting a women's movement of their own while they consider new life-style options.

158   "The Hardships That Blue-Collar Women Face." *Business Week,* 14
      August 1978, pp. 86-88.
          Points out the hostility blue-collar women deal with, how many
new skills they must learn, and how much spunk it all takes.

159   Hatfield, Julie. "Women's Work Wear Is Hard to Find: Heavy
      Duty." *Boston Globe,* 8 March 1984, p. 45.
          The author uses the occasion of International Women's Day to
look at the fact that the available work clothes for women construction
workers, engineers, carpenters, and master electricians are limited
indeed. She discusses the efforts being make locally to change the
inventories.

160   Hedges, J., and Bemis, S. "Sex Stereotyping: Its Decline in Skilled
      Trades." *Monthly Labor Review* 97 (May 1974): 14-22.

161   "Helping the Women in the Skilled Trades." *New York Times,* 4
      December 1980, p. C3.
          About the beginning in autumn 1976 of the Women in the
Trades association in New York City. The organization, which as of
1980 had 400 members, provides educational and employment
information.

162   Hernandez, Ruth Robinson. *A Woman's Guide to Apprenticeship.* A
      special report prepared for the Women's Bureau, U.S. Department
      of Labor. Washington, D.C.: U.S. Government Printing Office, 1980,
      30 pp.
          Prepared when Alexis Herman was director of the Women's
Bureau, this report is an excellent introduction to the apprenticeship
system in the United States and the barriers and support systems
women will discover within it.

163   Hoffman, B.H. *McCall's,* December 1977, p. 52. "Women Who
      Wear Hardhats: Blue-Collar Workers Surveyed by Mary Walshok."
          A discussion of Mary Lindenstein Walshok's early research.

164   Howard, Elizabeth. "Searching for a Job in the Construction Industry: Some Tips for Women." Washington, D.C.: U.S. Department of Labor, Women's Bureau, November 1979, 4 pp.

Pamphlet developed by Elizabeth Howard, a union carpenter and consultant on women in construction.

165   Kane, Roslyn D. *Problems of Women in Apprenticeship.* Arlington, Va.: Rj Associates, 1977.

An important study by a consultant. Analyzes the many problem areas for women in apprenticeship, including background, admission, fellow workers and supervisors, chivalry, related instruction, retention, need for support services, and many others. Analyzes related issues and draws conclusions. Asks: Where did all the applicants go? This wide-ranging study examines a variety of women, different trades, the point system, job-placement problems, social networking and transportation, government regulations and selecting a trade. Makes excellent recommendations to a variety of government, industrial, and educational institutions.

166   Kentucky Commission on Human Rights. *Women Miners: Complaints of Sex Discrimination Force Coal Industry to End "Male Only" Tradition.* Staff report no. 86-4, edited by Jenny Montgomery. Frankfort: Kentucky Commission on Human Rights, June 1986, 28 pp.

This report summarizes over ten years of work by the commission, including challenges to the idea of "men's work," probable-cause determinations made, what superstitions actually prevented companies from hiring women, history of forced hiring goals, resurgence of initiation rites as a result of first complaints, history of women in the mines, how men were recalled before women after layoffs, and the progress women are continuing to make.

167   Kerr, Peter. "Woman's Work: Rarely Blue-Collar." *New York Times,* 23 July 1982, p. 12, col. 2.

About a conference at the New School for Social Research called "Women in Apprenticeship, Blue-Collar, and High-Technology Trades." The 160 participants agreed that entry into these fields is not easy. Cites the Federal Bureau of Labor Statistics research that indicates that women constitute 5.7 percent of the construction and maintenance painters in the nation, 1.6 percent of the electricians, and

0.4 percent of the plumbers and pipe fitters. The conference was one of a series being held across the country by the Women's Bureau of the U.S. Department of Labor.

168   Kleiman, Carol. "Dockworker Strained Just to Get Her Feet Wet." *Chicago Tribune,* 6 July 1984.

About Gretchen Williams, who comes from a long line of Norwegian sailors, and who has finally landed a job as a marine clerk for the American Presidential Line. Getting the job was difficult: among other things, it took a class-action suit against the Pacific Maritime Association.

169   Kleiman, Carol. "Tradition-Bound Blue-Collar World Finally Sees Its Barriers Crumbling." *Chicago Tribune,* 15 June 1987, p. 7.

An overly dramatic headline leads to an article about one woman, a theater major from Northwestern University, who works as a hauler of rental spotlights for rock concerts in Chicago.

170   Kleiman, Carol. "Trying to Bridge the Gap in Road Work Opportunity." *Chicago Tribune,* 24 March 1986, sec. 4, p. 10.

About the Southeast Women's Employment Coalition's special project: Women's Opportunities in Road Construction.

171   "Layoffs Forcing Thousands of Blue-Collar Women Back into Low-Paying World of 'Women's Work' Just after Making Rise in Heavy Industry." *Wall Street Journal,* 6 March 1985, p. 37, col. 4.

172   Lederer, Muriel. *Blue-Collar Jobs for Women.* New York: Dutton, 1979.

A guide to the variety of blue-collar jobs available to women at that time.

173   Lehmann, Phyllis. "Women Journey into the Skilled Trades." *Worklife,* August 1977, pp. 27-31.

Contains many photos and a table of the twelve occupations with the largest number of registered women apprentices at the end of 1976.

174   Limmet, Nancy. "Better Pay Driving Women to the Trades." *Boston Sunday Globe,* 31 July 1983, p. A23.

About the women in the Boston area who begin new careers by enrolling in a training program at the Women's Technical Institute (1255 Boylston Street, Boston, MA 02215) to learn technical and blue-collar jobs.

175   Marino, Gigi. "Following My Father's Footsteps to the Sea." *Tradeswomen* 6, no. 1 (Winter 1987): 20-26.

The author describes her father's "distinction of being the only sailor in our small, landlocked coal mining town in western Pennsylvania." She earned her Merchant Mariner's Document and went to work for Exxon aboard an oil tanker called the *Exxon Banner.*

This article recounts her experiences over five years with sexual harassment, basic tasks aboard ship, and her eventual decision to stop going to sea in order to devote more time to her writing.

176   Minister of Supply and Services Canada. *Women in Mining: The Progress and the Problems.* Mineral Policy Series, Mineral Bulletin MR 152. (Place): Energy Mines and Resources Canada, 1976, 17 pp.

Good Canadian bibliography.

177   "Ms. Blue Collar." *Time,* 6 May 1974, p. 80.

The article discusses the formation of the Coalition for Labor Union Women (CLUW), a new pragmatic offshoot of the women's liberation movement: blue-collar feminism. The differences between blue-collar and white-collar feminists are clarified, and comments from several women on whether unity or separation is desirable are included.

178   "Networking and Resources." *Tradeswomen* 5, no. 4 (Fall 1986): 19.

Lists thirteen contact organizations for women around the country who are carpenters breaking into the construction industry.

179   O'Farrell, Brigid. *Blue-Collar Workers: Workshop III on Expanding Career Options of Women.* Wellesley, Mass.: Wellesley College, Center for Research on Women, Project on Expanding Career Options of Women.

A twenty-eight-page booklet containing the problem statement, background materials, and recommendations of a workshop on blue-collar workers. An important resource.

180   O'Farrell, Brigid. "Women and Nontraditional Blue-Collar Jobs in the 1980's: An Overview." In *Women in the Workplace,* edited by Phyllis A. Wallace. Boston: Auburn House, 1982.

O'Farrell, long a champion of research on women in nontraditional, blue-collar sectors, presents a substantial look at trends and issues for women and their employers in the eighties. She emphasizes initiatives for employers in the article. Another strength of the chapter is the author's scrupulous bibliographical references. Researchers are well advised to follow her work carefully, as she has consistently produced work of importance.

181   Pascoe, Elizabeth Jane. "Why Women Choose Blue-Collar Jobs." *Woman's Day,* 27 September 1978, p. 30.

182   Pennsylvania Department of Education. *People at Work: A Directory of Pennsylvanians Employed in Jobs Nontraditional to Their Sex.* Harrisburg: Pennsylvania Department of Education, 1981.

Ideas for this publication were incorporated from Kansas State University Adult and Occupational Education Department, Manhattan, Kans., which published something called *Strategies Handbook for Us* with the *Kansas Directory of Nontraditional Workers.* This book is a directory to people in nontraditional fields which gives data such as their addresses, whether they will speak to groups, etc., organized by occupations and cross-referenced by counties in Pennsylvania. Categories include: agriculture, attorneys, construction and industry, cosmetology, preschool and other education, management and administration, the military, security and law enforcement, nursing and health care, office and clerical work, owners of businesses, physicians, chiropractors, veterinarians, professions and technical careers, and miscellaneous work.

For further information, contact Jacqueline Culka, Equity Coordinator, Vocational Education Equity Program, Pennsylvania Department of Education, P.O. Box 911, 333 Market Street, Harrisburg, PA 17108.

183   Pugh, Monica, et al. *Opening Trade Barriers: A Training Blueprint.* Fort Wayne: Fort Wayne Women's Bureau, 1979.

Jari Himes, training specialist, wrote in the preface to this 128-page booklet that "a scarcity of pre-apprenticeship training programs and training materials for women led to the development of this book." It was designed to provide employment trainers and instructors with educational materials that can be used to prepare young women to enter apprenticeship or advanced training programs in the skilled trades. Manual describes basic classroom exercises used to sharpen required skills of apprenticeship candidates. Intentional emphasis on clarifying expectations and developing work behavior strategies with women who are interested in occupations still considered nontraditional for their gender.

184   Rabbinowitz, Allen. "Plumbers with a Twist: Missy Moscowitz, Plumber." *Ms.*, October 1986, pp. 62-64, 94.

About a father-and-daughter team of plumbers.

185   Samson, Stacie. "Women in the Trades." *Bay Windows*, 8 April 1987.

Published in New England's largest gay and lesbian newspaper, this lengthy cover story discusses the many Boston-area women, both gay and straight, who are moving into the building trades. They either work mostly with men on hard-hat construction sites, or they run their own companies such as Pipelines Inc., a woman-owned plumbing company. The author interviewed nine union and independent tradeswomen for the article and included the following jobs in construction: union carpenter, electrical apprentice, MBTA repairer, painter, and plumber.

186   Skilled Jobs for Women, Inc. *The Road Out from Under: An Action Plan for Moving Women Up in the Labor Force.* Madison, Wis.: Skilled Jobs for Women, Inc., 1977.

Includes chapters entitled "New Visions for Women's Work," "Redefining Woman's Place," and "Future Visions and Present Strategies." Also contains an essay on feminist values in the workplace.

187 Soltow, Martha Jane, and Werz, Mary K. *American Women and the Labor Movement, 1825-1974: An Annotated Bibliography.* Metuchen, N.J.: Scarecrow, 1976.
Historical role of women in American labor unions.

188 Tabor, Martha. "Working on the Railroad." *Off Our Backs,* October 1978, pp. 6-17.
Tabor writes of two women who work on the Boston and Maine Railroad. She includes "Thoughts on Women in the Blue-Collar Trades" and "Truck Driving" in this series of descriptive biographical articles. Photographs by Martha Tabor throughout.

189 Tetrault, Jeanne. *Be Your Own Best Friend: Blue-Collar Jobs for Women: A Resource Guide.* Illustrated by Karen Sjoholm. Tucson, Ariz.: Tucson Women's Commission and New West Trails Publication Collective, 1982.
Published with funding from the National Institute of Corrections, U.S. Department of Justice. Tetrault's analysis includes sections entitled: "Blue-Collar Work: What Is It Like?"; "Apprenticeship for Women: What and How"; "On the Job"; "Women and Blue-Collar Work: Questions and Answers"; and "Resources to Help You Choose a Trade." Utilizes a question-and-answer format; also contains lots of personal quotations.

190 "Tina Trades in Male-Only Rule." *Advertiser* [Adelaide, South Australia], 21 July 1987.
About a young woman in South Australia named Tina Miljanovic who works as a nursery supervisor in local botanic gardens. She is a member of a group called "Tradeswomen on the Move" who make six-week tours in South Australia to encourage teenage girls to consider the possibility of careers in nontraditional areas. Others in her group include a carpenter, a mechanic, a fitter and turner, and a horticulturalist. Miljanovic encourages girls to think of green keeping, tree surgery, contract lawn mowing, and floriculture. She points out that after some basic experience women can study botany and become

involved in research. The women travel in a bright yellow bus emblazoned with the words "Tradeswomen on the Move"; they travel to metropolitan schools for a week, and then they cover schools in the southeast, mid-south, the Riverland, and the far west regions of South Australia.

191   [Ullyot, J.] "Are Women Stronger Than Men?" *Harper's Bazaar,* May 1977, p. 89.

192   "Unwed Mothers Learning a Trade." *New York Times,* 26 July 1985, pp. 23-24.
    Discusses a program to expand options for teenage mothers in the New York City school system. The young mothers are receiving training for nontraditional jobs.

193   "U.S. Adopts Construction Hiring Goals for Women." *Monthly Labor Review* 101 (July 1978): 45.
    Nationwide goals for hiring women on construction projects, ranging from 3.1 percent of a project's work hours in the first year to 6.9 percent in the third year, are discussed. The U.S. Department of Labor adopted regulations intended to ensure employment opportunity and set legal procedures to address compliance, not only in hiring but also in promoting minorities and women. Compliance with Executive Order 11246, which called for equal opportunity and affirmative action, has strengthened by these efforts.

194   U.S. Department of Labor. Manpower Administration. Bureau of Apprenticeship and Training. *Apprenticeship: Past and Present.* Washington, D.C.: U.S. Government Printing Office, 1969, 23 pp.

195   U.S. Department of Labor. Women's Bureau. "A Woman's Guide to Apprenticeship." Washington, D.C.: U.S. Government Printing Office, 1978, 24 pp.
    Basic information provided to women to promote interest in apprenticeships.

196   U.S. Equal Employment Opportunity Commission (EEOC). *Minorities and Women in Referral Units in Building Trade Unions.* U.S. EEOC Research Report, no. 44. Washington, D.C.: U.S. Government Printing Office, 1974.

Covers asbestos workers, boilermakers, bricklayers, carpenters, elevator constructors, ironworkers, laborers, marble polishers, operating engineers, painters, plasterers, plumbers, pipe fitters, roofers, and sheet-metal workers.

197   Walshok, Mary Lindenstein. *Blue-Collar Women: Pioneers on a Male Frontier.* Garden City, N.Y.: Doubleday, Anchor Press, 1981.

Walshok interviewed 117 women, 34 of whom came from the San Francisco Bay Area, 70 from San Diego, and 13 from Los Angeles. The women worked in welding, carpentry, mechanics, and machining. She was interested in the family and childhood contexts that provide women with the baseline experiences and capabilities that in turn give them the potential to take risks and pursue nontraditional interests. She points out how women in blue-collar jobs have been overlooked in the research literature. She also explains why she thinks there is so much to learn from them. Through this book, Walshok tried to challenge some of the social stereotypes about blue-collar women.

198   Walshok, Mary Lindenstein. "Occupational Values and Family Roles: A Descriptive Study of Women Working in Blue-Collar and Service Occupations." *Urban and Social Change Review: Special Issue on Women and Work* 11 (1978): 12-20.

Walshok offers an overview of what is currently known about working-class women and working-class work based on census data and the body of published research results. Then she discusses emergent findings from her own research.

She is exploring the significance of paid employment to women entering nontraditional blue-collar occupations such as welding and auto mechanics. Her findings reveal the high significance of their work to the women but a simultaneous rejection or mixed support from significant others in their personal lives.

199   West, Karen. "How to Get a Blue Collar." *Ms.,* May 1977, pp. 62-65.

Interviews with three women exploring the higher wages, the sense of self-sufficiency, and the satisfaction of building something that endures.

200   Wheat, Valerie, and Niebel, Christie. *Apprenticeship and Other Blue-Collar Job Opportunities for Women.* San Francisco: Far West Laboratory for Educational Research and Development, 1978, 31 pp.

   Contains useful resources list, pp. 21-28. For full annotation, see entry 206.

201   White, Connie L., ed. *Coal Employment Project [CEP] Training Manual.* Oak Ridge, Tenn.: CEP, 1979.

   A lengthy introduction to what a woman must know to become an effective coal miner. For further information, contact CEP, 17 Emory Place, Knoxville, TN 37917.

202   Whittemore, Hank. "I Want Respect, That's All." *Parade Magazine,* 10 July 1988, pp. 4-5.

   An informative article about the more than 100,000 women who now drive big trucks for a living, published in the syndicated and popular Sunday-newspaper insert *Parade,* which is read by millions of people across the nation. The women are unified by their love of economic independence, the great outdoors, and physical labor. They seem to share experiences with sexual harassment, a desire to be taken seriously, and a desire to demonstrate their mastery of their chosen work.

203   Wilkinson, Carroll Wetzel. "A Critical Guide to the Literature of Women Miners." *Labor Studies Journal* 10, no. 1 (Spring 1985): 25-45.

   A comprehensive analysis of the books, articles, films, songs, and other resources available to date regarding women who live and work as miners in the United States.

204   "Women Back Ruling on Building Trades." *Chicago Tribune,* 6 January 1984.

   Brief article noting that a coalition of Chicago women who work in the building trades urge strict enforcement of a recently passed city ordinance. This ordinance requires that 50 percent of the workers on municipal building contracts be city residents and advocates increased hiring of women and minorities.

205 "Women in Traditionally Male, Blue-Collar Jobs." *Women: A Journal of Liberation* 4, no. 2 (Spring 1975).
Interviews with a bricklayer, truck driver, telephone coin collector, and auto mechanic.

206 Women's Educational Equity Communications Network (WEECN). *Apprenticeship and Other Blue-Collar Job Opportunities for Women.* San Francisco: WEECN, 1978, 31 pp.
An effort to educate women about apprenticeship opportunities. For more information, contact WEECN, 1855 Folsom Street, San Francisco, CA 94103.

207 "Women Seek Road Jobs, Not Road Blocks." *Monitor,* December 1984.
This article concerns the issues raised at a press conference in Washington, D.C., in mid-October of 1984 by the Southeast Women's Employment Coalition. The press conference was part of a strategy by SWEC to publicize their Women's Opportunities in Road Construction Project. Article contains a "Fact Sheet on Women's Employment in Road Construction."

208 "Women Win Considerable Acceptance as Stagehands in New York City." *New York Times,* 23 Sept 1987, sec. 3, p. 19, col. 1.
Although they account for only 1 percent of the membership of Local One of the Theatrical Protective Union, women are finding good work backstage in the theaters of New York City. In this article they comment on working in what has always been a male bastion and on what some of their experiences have been.

209 Yount, Kristen R. "Women and Men Coal Miners: Coping with Gender Integration Underground." Ph.D. dissertation, University of Colorado at Boulder, 1986.
Yount states that her central research purpose was to initiate a theoretical understanding of the integration of women into traditionally male, physical-labor jobs. Her primary sources of data are in-depth interviews with women and men who work in underground coal mines and company personnel and field notes collected during participant observation work in mining communities. She explores the relationship between conditions of production and modes of interaction in

underground mines. She addresses situational and individual factors affecting the integration of women into the workplace. She discusses a gender-based division of labor in which women are concentrated in low-prestige laborer positions. She summarizes the processes involved in undermining a woman's work reputation and self-concept, and she discusses forms of discrimination that recreate aspects of the female stereotype and lead to the development of sex segregation. Lengthy relevant bibliography is included, pp. 694-764. This dissertation is a major contribution to our understanding of the workplace dynamics for women in male-dominated blue-collar jobs. Some of her conclusions about coping behavior have interesting parallels to denial behavior of women in professional jobs in male-dominated fields. She points out that "in the face of danger, discomfort and dismal physical surroundings, miners cope with anxiety and frustration by maintaining self-presentations as competent, tough, and jocular, thereby indicating to each other, first, that the environment is benign and tolerable, and second, that they are capable of dealing with it."

Carpenters and Construction Industry Workers

210   "Atlanta Woman Helps Build Subway Station." *New York Times,* 8 September 1977, p. 46.

UPI release noting that Margo George of Atlanta feels a sense of accomplishment when she finishes a day's work as a carpenter for the Rapid Transit Authority. She mentions that her parents were both lawyers and they were not happy when she dropped out of the University of California at Berkeley to become an apprentice.

211   Cooke, Mary. "On the Job with a Welder Named Desire." *Honolulu Advertiser,* 4 March 1971.

A portrait of Desire Brooks, in 1971 the only woman member of the Hawaii chapter of the American Welding Society. She has been certified for Heliarc welding on aluminum, stainless steel, and exotic metals for eighteen years. (Heliarc welding is an arc welding process in which the weld area is shielded by an inert gas to prevent oxidation.) Excellent photograph included with article.

212   Dullea, George. "Women Win Fight for More Construction Jobs, Less Harassment." *New York Times,* 23 August 1977, p. C30.

Describes the goals and timetables actions of the U.S. Labor Department in its responses to lawsuits from women's groups; also points out the provision in the regulations that contractors "ensure and maintain a working environment free of harassment, intimidation, and coercion."

213   Ferretti, Fred. "Six Women Find Hard Hats Are a Good Fit." *New York Times,* 13 January 1984, p. B6.

     A biographical portrait of six women in construction jobs in New York City, their apprenticeships and adjustments, and their families' reactions.

214   Foreman, Judy. "Construction Women Not Women's Libbers." *Boston Globe,* 13 September 1978, p. 45.

     A spokesperson for NAWIC (National Association of Women in Construction) has said recently that of its 8,000 members, none are "women's libbers." "We have taken no note of and have no policy on the Equal Rights Amendment." Furthermore, they are opposed to the set of goals and timetables that has been set up by the U.S. Department of Labor for contractors who do business with the federal government. As might be expected, this is not an organization that represents blue-collar laboring women. Final quotation in article is: "Recalling one female carpenter in Texas, women in construction jobs have to be outside in all weather, and that can be hard on the hands and the complexion."

215   German, Eleanor. "Woman Carpenter Just Being Herself." *Christian Science Monitor,* 28 February 1979.

     The last in a series on men and women in nontraditional jobs, this is a profile of an Edgewater, Florida, woman named Ellie Lackey who is living her life the way it pleases her most – being a carpenter.

216   "Hardhats and Manholes: Not for Men Only." *Christian Science Monitor,* 27 March 1980, p. 19.

     A profile of a woman who had been with the New York Telephone Company for twenty years as an administrative clerk and who then enrolled in the company's Ultimate Goals Program, started in 1970. She is now a cable-splicing forewoman and the boss of a crew of six to ten splicers who repair the aerial, underground, and submarine cables linking telephone central offices to customers' homes and business locations.

217   "Ideas and Trends: Women on the Job–In Construction." *New York Times,* 28 August 1977, p. E6.

A brief mention is made in this article that the Department of Labor has proposed regulations that set goals and timetables for all building employers holding federal contracts or subcontracts of more than $10,000. If the regulations go into effect, an estimated 90,000 new jobs would open up to women in the next three years.

218   [Interview with Mary Ewing, carpenter.] In *Conversations: Working Women Talk about Doing a "Man's Job,"* edited by Terry Wetherby. Millbrae, Calif.: Les Femmes Press, 1977.

Ewing gives insight into her love of working with wood. (See entry 131 for full annotation on book.)

219   McCormick, Dale. *Against the Grain: A Carpentry Manual for Women.* Iowa City: Iowa City Women's Press, 1977.

An introduction to the challenges a woman carpenter faces.

220   Mechanical Contractors Association of America. *Guidelines for the Employment of Women in the Construction Industry.* Washington, D.C.: Mechanical Contractors Association of America, 1976, 26 pp.

Not particularly progressive, but gives guidelines to women who want to try to integrate the construction industry.

221   Morgan, Carol Lee. "A Day in the Work Life of Thomasina McClain, Cement Mason's Apprentice." *Women's Work,* September-October 1976, pp. 16-20.

McClain is a two-year apprentice in the Cement Masons, Local No. 891 program. She works in Washington, D.C., with a handful of other female cement masons as they construct the city's new metro. The article contains a photographic survey of the places in which she works. Photographs by Marianne Pernold. Seven black and white photos are included.

222   Morris, Stephen. "As Building Industry Grows, So Does the Role of Women." *Chicago Tribune,* 12 July 1985.

About several members of the National Association of Women in Construction, a group formed in 1955 with members in a variety of positions in the construction industry including architects, secretaries, trade-journal reporters, engineers, accountants, and building-material suppliers.

223   Powers, Karen Janes. "Building Skills from the Ground Up: Women Learn a Building Trade." *Ms.,* May 1986, p. 39.

About women in training as carpenters in California.

224   Rapoport, Daniel. "Building a Bridge to the New World of Women in Construction Work." *Washington Post,* 26 December 1980, p. A2.

Coverage of the city of Seattle's ambitious goal to build a major bridge with a work force that is at least 20 percent female. The article details the city's previous achievements in nontraditional work for women dating back to the Northwest frontier tradition and the deep involvement of women in defense department plant work in World War II. Rapoport also discusses the work of Marilyn Halvorson, founder and sole owner of The Wild Norwegian, a heavy-welding and structural-steel firm. She had just won a $395,000 subcontract to work on the new bridge.

225   Rappoli, Rick. "That's a 25-Year-Old Blond under That Hard Hat!" *Malden* [Massachusetts] *Evening News,* 19 March 1979, p. 17.

A lengthy article about one of seventy-five women in construction jobs in the whole state of Massachusetts. At the time, she was working for Volpe Constructions at the site of a new chemistry laboratory at Harvard University.

226   Snyder, Sarah. "Women Now Looking to New Jobs in Construction." *Boston Globe,* 25 November 1986, pp. 17, 24.

About the renewal of a defunct Boston-area program called "Homes in the Building Trades." Statistics are included about the numbers of women who were then working as plumbers, electrical workers, etc. Women held an estimated 3-4 percent of the 13,000 construction jobs in Boston as of 1986, according to the article.

227   "Women Construction Worker Quotas." *New York Times,* 8 April
1978, p. 24.
        A UPI release announcing that the Labor Department set
quotas on 8 April 1978 for hiring of women as construction workers on
federal projects. The initial goal was to make the number of women
workers 3.1 percent of the total work force on federal construction
projects by mid-1979.

228   *A World of Opportunity in Construction.* Fort Wayne: Northeastern
Indiana Construction Advancement Foundation, 1977, 41 pp.
        A booklet encouraging career choices in the construction
industry for women.

Fire Fighters

Of all the hotbeds of rampant sex discrimination examined in this study, the
world of fire fighting is the most perplexing. Especially in New York City the
conflict between men and women has deepened and become more bitter as
time has passed. The literature reveals that women fight fires in rural areas
effectively and competently without the vicious criticism and misogyny that is
seen in some metropolitan areas. Men's fear of women, their intense
defensiveness in reaction to the women's willingness to face danger, and their
absolute opposition to women's integration is a theme throughout this
literature. Extreme, life-threatening danger is also faced by coal miners,
pilots, astronauts, and construction workers, but male workers in these fields
seem to have adjusted better than their fire-fighting counterparts to women's
competence and mastery. Why has this social progress not been possible in
urban fire fighting?

229   "All-Women Fire Force–In Texas, Naturally." *New York Times,* 2
January 1973, p. 40.
        Woodbine, Texas, population 500, is sixty miles north of Fort
Worth. Several local women founded the volunteer fire department
after an unusually dry spell that caused many serious brush fires. The
women got together enough money to buy a truck and they went into
business after appropriate training. The article contains several
amusing anecdotes about fires successfully doused and adventures with
the truck's reverse gear.

230   Buder, Leonard. "Judge Bars Bias by Fire Fighters." *New York Times,* 14 June 1986, p. 32.

Judge Sifton ruled again on behalf of women fire fighters by issuing an order that kept a Queens company from transferring Katrina Cannon, one of the first women fire fighters in New York City. Cannon became a fire fighter in 1982.

231   "Chief Denies Iowa Firemen Were Sexist." *New York Times,* 25 January 1984, p. C8.

Linda Eaton, the fire fighter who got a court order to allow her to breast-feed her baby at the fire station, filed a $940,000 discrimination suit against the fire chief and other officials in Iowa City. The chief discusses what male chauvinism is in this article, and he says all he ever saw were efforts to be chivalrous to the woman.

232   Cooper, Dr. Zachary L., and Hay, Gloria A. *Firefighter Pretraining Program.* Madison, Wis.: Madison Urban League (MUL).

Brief booklet on the program including the Madison, Wisconsin, Fire Department and the MUL–women were among the recruits. The booklet shows an unusual sensitivity to the issues involved in training women to be fire fighters.

233   Crockett, Sandra. "Fire Hopefuls Hanging Around for Agility Test." *Chicago Tribune,* 12 August 1985.

Smokebusters Inc., a black fire fighters' association in Chicago, is training fire fighter hopefuls for the agility tests. The article describes the training program, which has a small but energetic group of women in it.

234   Daley, Suzanne. "Female Fire Fighters Charge Inaction on Sex Bias." *New York Times,* 18 June 1986, p. B2.

Brenda Berkman, president of the United Women Fire Fighters, testified at a city council hearing on employment opportunities for women in the uniformed services, and she was joined by representatives of the Women in Transit Police.

235   Daley, Suzanne. "Sex Bias Lingers in Firehouses of New York." *New York Times,* 8 December 1986, pp. A1, B6.

Four years after the 13,000-member department hired its first women under court order, according to this article, overt acts of harassment – such as physical assault, urine in their boots, and firecrackers under their beds – have declined. But discrimination against the women continues, and a deep resentment against the women is prevalent among the men. Daley points out that Fire Commissioner Joseph E. Spinnato announced on 1 July 1986 that a series of departmentwide steps should be taken to modify the hostility. The steps included sensitivity training for 650 officers, hiring of a consultant to develop an overall approach to the problem, and formation of an advisory committee on sexual discrimination. But five months later there were signs that the commitment to these efforts was less than dedicated. This is a lengthy and probing article that provides a rational perspective on why the difficulties in New York have prevailed for such an unreasonable length of time. Views of Terry Floren, head of Women in Fire Suppression in Toledo, Ohio, are included.

236 Dunlap, David W. "Firemen Wary about Role for Women." *New York Times*, 8 February 1982, pp. B1, B12.

Dunlap talked to New York men in their firehouses about women joining their ranks, and this article outlines his findings.

237 Dunlap, David W. "Women Accepted as Fire Fighters." *New York Times*, 14 April 1982.

In Newark, there is one fire fighter who is a woman, and she is black. Jacquelin Jones is in a group of 647, and she has been accepted very well, according to Dunlap. The Newark fire fighters' behavior is in direct contrast to the open resistance to women on the part of the New York City firemen.

238 "Fire Department Criticized on Harassment." *New York Times*, 15 January 1987, sec. 2, p. 5, col. 1.

Brief text explaining that testimony had been given the day before to the New York City Council's Committee on Women about the fact that the "Fire Department had not done enough to combat sexual harassment on the job." There was acknowledgment that some progress, however, had been made. Article includes photo by Edward Hausner of fire fighters Brenda G. Berkman and Joann Jacobs.

239   Floren, Terry. "What's the Difference between Male and Female Fire Fighters?" *Tradeswoman* 4, no. 2 (Spring 1985): 10.

Puts forward the idea that female fire fighters are more likely to be downwardly mobile; that is, they tend to come from middle-class backgrounds, whereas most of the men come from the working class. She discusses the conflicts this produces in the workplace.

240   Fried, Joseph P. "Women Win Ruling on Fire Department Test." *New York Times,* 6 March 1982, pp. 1, 10.

Article about Judge Charles P. Sifton's ruling that a physical test for applicants to New York City's Fire Department discriminates against women. The judge ruled that a new test must be developed and thus angered Nicolas Mancuso, president of the Uniformed Fire Fighters Association, who interpreted the ruling to mean that a reduction in standards for the job was mandated. The judge ordered that forty-five women must be appointed.

241   Galvan, Manuel, and Crawford, William B., Jr. "Fire Fighter Hirings Delays Pending Test." *Chicago Tribune,* 15 September 1985.

Officials were refusing to hire from the 21,522 candidates who took the written exam until the physical tests were given.

242   "It Will Be Nice to See More Female Fire Fighters." *Chicago Defender,* 11 October 1986.

Editorial on the twenty-one women who were training to become fire fighters in Chicago. Among other points in this editorial, the writer says that fires don't restrict themselves to certain parts of the city – they are everywhere, and the best talent possible is needed to fight them.

243   Jamison, Pat. "First Firepersons Graduate." *Chicago Defender,* 31 January 1987.

About the twenty women graduating from the Chicago Fire Academy. Seven of the graduating women were black.

244   Keerdoja, Eileen. "Firewomen: Still Sparking Controversy." *Newsweek,* 7 March 1983, p. 9.

There are now about 450 women out of 180,000 paid fire fighters in the country. This article describes some of the places they are working.

245   Kiernan, Laura. "Miss Devlin Dropped as a Firefighter." *Washington Post,* 12 November 1974, p. C5.

The acting city manager of Alexandria City fired the city's first woman fire fighter, and this article documents the events leading up to and following the dismissal.

246   Kihss, Peter. "Fire Department, in Court Pact, Makes Room for Women." *New York Times,* 8 December 1980, sec. 2, p. 3, col. 2.

About the fact that New York City's Fire Department has reserved twenty-five places for women as probationary fire fighters, but it will only offer the jobs if forced by a federal judge.

247   Mancuso, Nicolas. "On Fitness Standards: Testing Female Fire Fighters." Letter to the editor. *New York Times,* 4 September 1982.

The president of the Uniformed Fire Fighters Association expresses his view that letting women become fire fighters will lower the standards.

248   "Mostly Female Fire Fighters Serve at Naval Air Station, Adak, Alaska." *Minerva: Quarterly Report on Women and the Military* 4, no. 4 (Winter 1986): 40.

249   Prial, Frank J. "Twenty-four Women Take Physical Test for Fire Department and Sixteen Pass It." *New York Times,* 9 September 1982, p. 1, col. 2.

The author describes the five-year battle predating this breakthrough, and she discusses the implications for the fire department and the successful women. The article contains several excellent photographs. One, by Sara Kailwich of the *New York Times,* expresses the joy of three women who had just learned they had passed the fire fighter's physical examination.

250   Richard, Ray. "Lexington Fire Fighter Adjusts – Now She's One of the Guys." *Boston Globe,* 10 November 1981, p. 2.

Ann Pastreich, a Phi Beta Kappa scholar in college, was the only female fire fighter who had a permanent appointment in Massachusetts at the time of the article. She was then 39 years old and was described as feeling less sensitive about her work after she began to blend in and lose her high visibility.

251 Schanberg, Sydney H. "My Little Sex Object." *New York Times,* 6 March 1984.

Schanberg discusses a song performed in the Inner Circle's annual lampoon show in front of 1,700 dinner guests at the Hilton Hotel. The song satirized Brenda Berkman and Federal Judge Sifton's actions that forced the fire department to admit women in 1982. There was a negative reaction to the song and many felt it was tasteless and inappropriate, going beyond the boundaries of satire.

252 Shute, Nancy. "NASM Has a Jump on Forest Fires for Its New Exhibit." *Smithsonian* 15 (March 1985): 167-71.

This article contains a biographical portrait of Linda Reimers, a smoke jumper for the U.S. Forest Service and, simultaneously, a director and filmmaker for the National Air and Space Museum. She was responsible for a five-minute film on aerial fire fighting for an exhibition at the Smithsonian in 1985. The article outlines the kind of training she was required to undergo, and it also sketches a history of the airborne fire fighters that begins in 1919.

253 Stabiner, Karen. "The Storm over Women Fire Fighters." *New York Times Magazine,* 26 September 1982, sec. 6, p. 100.

Stabiner covers the successes of Barbara Beers in Seattle and the resistance in many other cities across the nation to women fire fighters. She points out that this is combat duty and the military flatly denies women the right to participate. She also points out women must be physically strong to do the work of fire fighting. And beyond that they must have determination. She says: "Fire fighting, for women, is more than a test of physical strength and endurance; it is a psychological marathon as well."

254 Strausberg, Chinta. "Urge Women to Join the Fire Department." *Chicago Defender,* 1 May 1985.

Chicago's only female fire fighter speaks out to encourage other women to take the upcoming fire fighter's exam. In Chicago, there are a total of 4,504 people on the fire-fighting force.

255   Taylor, Marianne. "Women Fire Up to Test for Department." *Chicago Tribune,* 17 April 1985.
About the training women in Chicago are undergoing to become fire fighters.

256   "Two Sisters Are Doing What Comes Naturally: Fighting Fires in Illinois." *New York Times,* 25 November 1977.
In an unincorporated town, Clarendon Heights, Illinois, two sisters who grew up in a fire station because their father was a fire chief have joined the volunteer force. They are trained in all aspects of fire fighting and are working toward licenses to drive the fire trucks.

257   Vecsey, George. "Firemen Shortage Sparks Women to Train." *New York Times,* 24 May 1973.
In Nissequogue, Long Island, in 1973, fourteen women volunteered and were trained to be fire fighters. The article is interesting as a period piece because the photographs included are of women looking very tentative in their new gear. One small photo shows a woman being overcome by smoke. Vecsey's most memorable quote is: "The women trainees worked in a controlled fire in an abandoned cottage last Sunday with eyes watering and make-up disturbed."

Professions

The differential treatment of women in the work force most directly violates the principle of equality of opportunity because it affects people who have established, by virtue of obtaining an advanced degree, the right to pursue a scientific or engineering career based solely on the quality of their work. It also has a significant discouraging effect on female students in the educational pipeline, who see the future benefits of their investment in science and engineering education eroded by potential unemployment and underutilization in the work force.

> —Federal Office of
> Technology Assessment,
> From report to the House
> Committee on Science and
> Technology, 1985

As so many others have pointed out, women in the high-prestige professions have been observed, interviewed, studied, and commented on most vigorously for almost twenty years. This literature documents that fact and gives insight into real advances as well as persistent problems for women at work as, for example, scientists, surgeons, lawyers, and engineers.

General Studies and Miscellaneous Professions

258   Albertson, Joann. "You're Qualified, but You're Female." *Journal of College Placement* 30, no. 1 (October-November 1969): 37.
About the difficulties in the late 1960s of applying for a job in nuclear engineering if you were a woman. The article is written by a young woman in her senior year in college.

259   "Another Funeral for Discrimination against Women." *S/A: The Magazine of San Antonio, Texas* 3, no. 11 (January 1980): 20-22.
A profile of Mary Hugler, a black woman who is a mortician.

260   "Attila the Nun Is First Woman Attorney General." *Chicago Tribune,* 6 December 1984, p. 48.
On 1 January 1985 in Rhode Island, Arlene Violet, a former nun, became the first woman ever elected a state attorney general in the United States. She earned her law degree in the early 1970s after

teaching in parochial schools in the 1960s. Her zeal for social justice issues won her this nickname.

261   Beil, C., Sisk, D. R., and Miller, W. E. "A Comparison of Specialty Choices among Senior Medical Students Using the Bem Sex-Role Inventory Scale." *Journal of the American Medical Women's Association* 35 (1980): 178-81.

This study examines reasons female medical students avoid some specialties and gravitate toward others. Using the Bem Sex-Role Inventory Scale, the authors conclude that self-perceptions regarding sex role are poor indicators of specialty choice except in cases of pediatrics and surgery.

262   Brozan, Nadine. "For Female M.D.'s: Success at a Price." *New York Times,* 16 April 1986.

About a conference at Hunter College called "Women in Medicine: Challenges of the Future." Mentions more women are found now in fields where their entry has traditionally been discouraged: surgery, urology, and orthopedics.

263   Burlew, Ann Kathleen. "The Experiences of Black Females in Traditional and Nontraditional Professions." *Psychology of Women Quarterly* 6, no. 3 (Spring 1982): 312-26.

The author investigated the differences in the backgrounds, attitudes, and career-related expectations of black college females pursuing traditional and nontraditional careers. She studied a sample of 147 black women who were attending an urban university in the Midwest. Her research findings are blended in this article with an important literature review on career options for black professional women as of 1982. (For further annotation, see entry 599.)

264   Burns, Jim, and Brown, Betty Ann. *Women Chefs: A Collection of Portraits and Recipes from California's Culinary Pioneers.* Berkeley, Calif.: Aris Books, 1987.

This book focuses on the empowerment of women in the commercial kitchen. It contains photographs of the women in the kitchens where they are in control, and it also includes many recipes. The book contains an introductory essay tracing the history of women's exclusion until recently from positions of power in the food industry.

265   Claiborne, Craig. "Three Chefs Succeeding in a Man's World." *New York Times,* 6 November 1985, pp. 17, 19.

Article about three female French chefs. One comments: "The greatest problem for female chefs may not involve discrimination in the daily tasks of kitchen duty, but discouragement by the profession." She said she could not name a single woman who, in a kitchen run by a man, had been promoted to the rank of *chef de cuisine.* "The only way for a woman to become a chef is to open her own establishment."

266   Cuca, J. M. "The Specialization and Career Preferences of Women and Men Recently Graduated from U.S. Medical Schools." *Journal of the American Medical Women's Association* 34 (1979): 425-35.

When the students were asked their reasons for choosing one specialty over another, the typical reasons given were opportunities for self-fulfillment, positive clinical experiences, an intellectual challenge, and a favorable type of patient. Perceptions of gender tracking did not exist.

267   DiPerna, Paula. "A Third Mate Named Susan." *Collegiate Career Woman* 8, no. 3 (Spring 1981): 11-15.

About Susan Janis, the only woman officer on the *Exxon Boston,* a 52,000-ton deadweight oil tanker; she is a graduate of the State University of New York Maritime Academy at Fort Schuyler. Includes many photographs of Ms. Janis at work.

268   Ducker, P. "Believed Suitability of Medical Specialties for Women Physicians." *Journal of the American Medical Women's Association* 33 (1978): 25-32.

Shows that sexual bias does exist among faculty as to specialty suitability for their students. When asked which specialties they would recommend to men and women, 84-percent-male faculty, regardless of personal specialty, made different recommendations for women and men.

269   Dullea, George. "Women Win the Prize of Law Partnership." *New York Times,* 25 February 1985, sec. 2, p. 5, col. 2.

About several successful women in law firms who have achieved partnerships and some of the issues raised by their promotions to these positions of power.

270   Easton, Susan, et al. *Equal to the Task: How Working Women Are Managing in Corporate America.* New York: Seaview Books, 1982.

Identifying four prototypical women in business, this book discusses the assimilated woman, the autocratic woman, the alienated woman, and the ambivalent woman. The authors suggest that all of these prototypes are caused by trying to fit into a male world and that their overall effect is to limit individuality.

271   Ensrud, Barbara. "The Romance and Science of Winemaking: Meet the First Generation of Women Vintners." *Ms.*, August 1985, pp. 58.

About the American women who now earn their living as enologists or winemakers. Starting in 1973 and primarily operating out of California at both small and large wineries, these women have integrated this occupation, which was for so long considered "for men only." Bucking folklore that suggested that a menstruating woman could contaminate the wine by her mere presence, approximately ten have enrolled and graduated each year from California university programs in enology since 1973. A woman named Mary Ann Gray was UC Davis's first enology graduate in 1965, so it was she who broke the gender barrier. The work requires a knowledge of basic chemistry, a sensitivity to the details of nurturing wine's development, and a love of physical labor.

272   Epstein, Cynthia Fuchs. *Woman's Place: Options and Limits in Professional Careers.* Berkeley: University of California Press, 1971.

An important and insightful study. An eminent sociologist's study of why what she calls "our best women–those in whom society has invested most heavily" underperform, underachieve, and underproduce.

The book is an analysis of why and how this happens in American high-prestige professions.

She points out: "The woman who has proved her capabilities in training cannot generally count on society for encouragement or her colleagues for fair treatment." Her analysis of the structure of professions in chapter 4 is particularly fascinating.

See entry 64 for further annotation.

273   Epstein, Cynthia Fuchs. "Women and Professional Careers: The Case of the Woman Lawyer." Ph.D. dissertation, Department of Sociology, Columbia University, 1968.

274 Epstein, Cynthia Fuchs. *Women in Law.* New York: Basic Books, 1981.

With reference to her dissertation research, completed in 1968, Epstein analyzes what has happened to women lawyers as a result of the dramatic social changes of the 1970s. This book describes the new women of law, their background, their experiences in somewhat transformed law schools, the kinds of jobs they have taken and the obstacles they have encountered, their personal lives, and the way they cope with the social dynamics they encounter professionally. In chapter 15 she writes of the "ambivalence and collegiality of being an outsider within." Her analysis is important because it tackles the impediments of culture, the notion of being a good woman, the consequences of sex typing, the dynamics of proving oneself, exclusion from the club, the politics of making conversation, role alternation, interpersonal work, maintaining social distance, class differences, sexuality in the professional context, ideological separateness, and reducing ambiguity. All of these subjects are discussed in detail with insight, and a real picture of the complexities of the legal profession for women emerges.

275 Fabricant, Florence. "A Prizewinning Sommelier." *Ms.,* August 1985, p. 62.

About Anne Marie Guaranta, the 1980 winner of the Best Young Professional Sommelier of the Year Award. She was the first woman in France ever to win this prestigious prize for wine stewards, and at eighteen she was also the youngest person ever to win.

276 Falkner, David. "An Umpire Calls Her Tune." *New York Times,* 26 July 1986, sec. 1, p. 46, col. 1.

Perry Lee Barber is an umpire, working for $30.00 per game through the summer season of a Westchester league made up of players chosen in the college draft and former minor leaguers. She is also a pop singer.

277 Farley, Jennie, ed. *The Woman in Management: Career and Family Issues.* Ithaca, N.Y.: Cornell University, Industrial and Labor Relations Press, 1983.

This book contains conference proceedings. Among the participants and speakers were Rosabeth Moss Kanter, Juanita Kreps, and Betty Harragan.

278   Ferrandez, John P. *Racism and Sexism in Corporate Life: Changing Values in American Business.* Lexington, Mass.: Lexington Books, 1981.

   Old-guard and new-guard managers' values are clarified and discussed.

279   Fowler, Elizabeth. "Electronics Field Offers Opportunity." ("Careers" column.) *New York Times,* 27 February 1980.

   About the serious labor shortage in this growing field. Mentions Bell and Howell as the largest trainer of electronics technicians and technologists. ITT has a school in Indianapolis, Electronics Institute and Penn Technical Institute in Pittsburgh, Lincoln Technical Institute in Pennsauken, N.J., United Electronics in Tampa Bay, Florida, the Technical Career Institute in New York, Connecticut School of Electronics in New Haven, National Technical School in Los Angeles. Fowler concludes there are great opportunities for women in these nontraditional occupations.

280   Gashiva, N. *Women's Annotated Legal Bibliography.* New York: Clark Berkman, 1984.

   Extensive section of citations on employment discrimination.

281   Gump, Janice Porter. "Sex-Role Attitudes and Psychological Well-Being." *Journal of Social Issues* 28 (1972):79-92.

   The article is based in part on the author's 1967 dissertation research on sex-role attitudes and their relationship to psychological well-being in 162 women attending the University of Rochester. She discusses her research finding that ego strength is inversely related to adoption of the female sex role and that more purposeful and resourceful women are less traditional in their sex-role orientation. Gump also discusses that small part of her sample entering the highly competitive, traditionally masculine fields of chemistry, medicine, molecular biology, and experimental and clinical psychology.

282   Hennig, Margaret, and Jardim, Ann. *The Managerial Women.* New York: Doubleday, Anchor Press, 1978.

   Legendary insights into women's experiences in the world of business.

283　Hill, Gladwin. "Now Hear This: A Woman Is Running the Ship." *New York Times,* 10 July 1979.

　　　Lieutenant Kathleen Edwards's tour of duty as second in command of the SS *Surveyor,* a 292-foot, 3,150-ton vessel in the research fleet of the National Oceanic and Atmospheric Administration, is discussed in this article written on board the ship off the coast of Alaska.

284　Horst, Jeffrey D. "The Application of Title VII to Law Firm Partnership Decisions: Women Struggle to Join the Club." *Ohio State Law Journal* 44, no. 3 (1983): 841-90.

　　　A thorough discussion of overcoming discrimination at the time of partnership decisions.

285　Kovacic, Candace S. "Applying a Restitution to Remedy a Discriminatory Denial of Partnership." *Syracuse Law Review* 34 (Summer 1983): 743-802.

　　　The author discusses the issue of denial of partnership in a large law firm to a woman. She presents an approach to a discriminatory decision that she thinks will remedy the injustice. The action is restitution in which a liability is based on the woman's firm's unjust enrichment during her years of employment. Her point is that Title VII should apply not only to entry-level nontraditional areas for women but also to the higher-level positions that represent power, authority, money, and prestige.

286　Lemkau, Jeanne Parr. "Personality and Background Characteristics of Women in Male-Dominated Professions." *Psychology of Women Quarterly* 4, no. 2 (Winter 1979): 221-40.

　　　See entry 90 for annotation.

287　Lorber, Judith. *Women Physicians: Careers, Status, and Power.* New York: Tavistock, 1984.

　　　Lorber explores the discrimination that women doctors experience as they pursue their careers in the male-dominated world of medicine.

288   Lorimer, Anne. "She Turned from Nursing to Driving Locomotive." *Christian Science Monitor,* 7 February 1979, p. 15.

Trained and employed by the Boston and Maine Railway, Ida Depani was one of four women locomotive engineers in the United States at that time.

289   Louviere, Vernon. "Women's Growing Role in Lobbying." *Nation's Business,* June 1978, pp. 80-85.

How women are seeking to influence legislation in Washington. Includes profiles of some of the new lobbyists.

290   Lyle, Jerolyn R., and Ross, Jane L. *Women in Industry: Employment Patterns of Women in Corporate America.* Lexington, Mass.: D.C. Heath & Co., Lexington Books, 1973.

The authors studied the relationships among thirty characteristics of 246 firms. They found that the largest firms with the most employees practice less occupational discrimination than do smaller or peripheral firms. The authors also discovered evidence of employee resistance to female supervisors.

291   McBroom, Patricia. *The Third Sex: The New Professional Woman.* New York: William Morrow & Co., 1986.

McBroom interviewed forty-four female financial executives in New York and San Francisco in order to understand the consequences "of collapsing gender worlds triggered by the mass movement of women into professional roles originally restricted to men." McBroom, an anthropologist, found that no aspect of women's lives was left unchanged by their integration into male-dominated fields. And she finds the changes are having an effect on men's lives as well. She organizes her findings into the following chapter topics: the gender cultures; women who reject motherhood; women who have children; women in the middle; and sex and corporations. She discusses the concepts of the masculine professional, gender transformations, and the masks women wear in their professional lives. She discusses image making, the price of careers, and the various characteristics of professional culture. A copy of the forty-seven question survey she used to gather her data is included. McBroom's exploratory, qualitative study is particularly interesting for its exploration of identity in an anthropological, rather than psychological, sense. Her analysis of acquired cultural identity is an important contribution to understanding one critical social factor women in nontraditional fields face.

292 McLane, Helen. *Selecting, Developing, and Retaining Women Executives: A Corporate Strategy for the Eighties.* New York: Van Nostrand Reinhold, 1980.
About affirmative-action strategies.

293 Mandelbaum, Dorothy Rosenthal. *Work, Marriage, and Motherhood: The Career Persistence of Women Physicians.* New York: Praeger, 1981.

294 Mattfeld, Jacquelyn A., and Van Aken, Carol G., eds. *Women and the Scientific Professions: The MIT Symposium on American Women in Science and Engineering.* Cambridge, Mass.: MIT Press, 1965.
Contains essays (originally given as talks at a conference) that address critical issues faced by women entering the scientific professions. Essay authors include Bruno Bettelheim, Erik Erikson, and many others. The conference raised many of the issues for scientifically gifted women still under discussion almost twenty-five years later. See full annotation in entry 404.

295 Merin, Jennifer. "Women Gain Ground as Officials." *USA Today,* 26 July 1983.
A lengthy discussion of women's slow but steady progress as officials in men's major-league sporting events in the United States. Betty Ellis and Rosalie Kramm's recognition by the North American Soccer League and Pam Postema and Bernice Gera's recognition by the Triple A Pacific Coast League in baseball are mentioned. The article points out that no major league's policy bars women, but women were not expected to try to integrate the macho worlds of the National Hockey League or the National Football League.

296 Morello, Karen Berger. *The Invisible Bar: The Woman Lawyer in America, 1638 to the Present.* Boston: Beacon Press, 1986.

A history in ten chapters of women in the legal profession in the United States. Chapter 6, pp. 143-72, deals exclusively with black women's history in the law.

297   "Panel Reports Sex Disparity for Engineers and Scientists." *New York Times,* 26 December 1985, sec. 1, p. 15, col. 1.

This article discusses a study done by the U.S. Office of Technology Assessment at the request of the House of Representatives' Committee on Science and Technology. The group was asked to consider the barriers to the participation of women and minorities in scientific occupations, among other factors. The survey report revealed that female scientists and engineers are paid less and receive fewer promotions than their male counterparts–and that they are also discouraged from taking scientific and technical jobs in the first place.

298   "Preparing Black Women for Nontraditional Professions: Some Considerations for Career Counseling." *National Association of Women Deans, Administrators, and Counselors Journal* 40, no. 4 (Summer 1977): 135-39.

Important insights into black women's unique experiences.

299   Psychological Barriers to Occupational Success for Women." *National Association of Women Deans, Administrators, and Counselors Journal* 40, no. 4 (Summer 1977): 140-43.

300   Roark, Anne C. "Women Scientists Treated Equitably, Sociologist Finds." *Chronicle of Higher Education* 19, no. 70 (5 November 1979): 1.

A review of Jonathan R. Cole's book *Fair Science: Women in the Scientific Community* (New York: Free Press, 1979).

301   Sherrod, Pamela. "Inventor's Grandchild Turns Mother of Invention." *Chicago Tribune,* 9 March 1987.

About Mary Louise O'Grady, a surgical nurse who designed three cardiac surgical instruments.

302 Sicherman, Barbara. *Alice Hamilton: A Life in Letters.* Cambridge, Mass.: Harvard University Press, Commonwealth Fund, 1984.

    A well-researched biography. Hamilton, who was born in 1869 and lived to be 101, was a trailblazer in many ways for women. She was a physician and reformer, the first woman professor at Harvard, and a pioneer in industrial medicine and toxicology. She is also considered by some to be the grandmother of the Occupational Safety and Health Administration. Hamiltion is an inspiring role model for women in all nontraditional fields.

303 Spencer, Jim. "A Challenge Met, A Goal Attained: From Trial Lawyer to Mother to Federal Judge." *Chicago Tribune,* 25 July 1985.

    Lengthy biography of Ann Williams, the first black federal judge appointed by President Ronald Reagan.

304 Steinem, Gloria. "Gro Harlem Bruntlands." *Ms.,* January 1988, pp. 74-75.

    A biographical sketch of a feminist pioneer who became the prime minister of Norway in 1981 and again in 1986. She is the author of *Our Common Future,* a book about environmental issues, and according to Steinem, she is a "leader in the mostly male world of futurists."

305 Tennison, Patricia. "Woman Chef Stands Kitchen Heat for Prize." *Chicago Tribune,* 1 February 1987.

    About Susan Weaver, sous-chef at Chicago's Ritz Carleton Hotel, who placed seventh out of twenty-four in a world-class cooking championship held in Bayonne, France.

306 Woman Is Seeking a Career as an Umpire." *New York Times,* 5 April 1975.

    A twenty-six-year-old woman named Christine Wren from Mission Hills, California, has announced her intention to become a major-league umpire. With a burst of enthusiasm she says, "Once you prove you are a good official, they don't care if you are black, white, male, or female."

Composers and Conductors

307   Ammer, Christine. *Unsung: A History of Women in American Music.* Westport, Conn.: Greenwood Press, 1980.

    Ammer introduces her book by saying, "Several years of research have shown that women have been writing and performing music for as long as men have. But owing to the social climate of earlier times their work went unnoticed, unpublished, unperformed, and was completely forgotten. This book is a history of the role played by women in American music, as performers, composers, and teachers." She covers both overt and subtle forms of discrimination against women in positions of authority in the world of music.

308   Apone, Carl. "Victoria Bond: Composer, Conductor." *High Fidelity/Musical America,* April 1979, pp. 28-29.

309   Bayia, Anne. "Antonia Brico." *Fugue,* October 1978, pp. 25-27.

310   Block, Adrienne, and Neuls-Bates, Carol, eds. *Women in American Music: A Bibliography of Music and Literature.* Westport, Conn.: Greenwood Press, 1976.

    The National Endowment for the Humanities as well as the Ford Foundation supported the creation of this book. It contains more than 5,000 entries on women in classical music.

311   Boroff, Edith. "Women Composers: Renaissance and History." *College Music Symposium* 15 (1975): 26-33.

312   Bowers, Jane, and Tick, Judith, eds. *Women Making Music: Studies in the Social History of Women Musicians and Composers.* Berkeley: University of California Press, 1982.

313 Claghorn, Jane. *Women Composers and Hymnists: A Concise Biographical Dictionary.* Metuchen, N.J.: Scarecrow Press, 1984.

314 Cohen, Aaron I., comp. *International Discography of Women Composers.* Westport, Conn.: Greenwood Press, 1984.

315 Cohen, Aaron I. *International Encyclopedia of Women Composers.* New York: R. R. Bowker, 1981.

316 Cornell, H. L. "An Evaluation of Vocal Music by American Women Composers As to Its Appropriateness in the Elementary School." Ph.D. dissertation, Ohio State University, 1973.

317 Dyer, Richard. "DeVaron's 30 Years in the Forefront." *Boston Globe,* 28 March 1978.
     The conductor of the choruses of the New England Conservatory asserts "of course being a woman held me back, you know that. When you are a conductor you are the supreme authority and people are bound to resent that when it is represented by a woman."

318 Ericson, Raymond. "Celebrating Louise Talma." *New York Times,* 4 February 1977.
     This composer has been writing and teaching at Hunter College for fifty years. Her prolific output is reviewed in this article.

319 Ericson, Raymond. "Miss Hillis Carries Her Baton Lightly." *New York Times,* 2 November 1977, p. 23.
     Ericson interviewed Margaret Hillis following her triumphant conducting success with the Chicago Symphony Orchestra at Carnegie Hall.

320   Ericson, Raymond. "She Waves a Baton at Adversity." *New York Times,* 7 January 1977.

In this article, conductor Eve Queler asserts that she has never experienced discrimination, though she is quoted as saying the following: "I know that some orchestra managers, when approached to engage me, have turned me down because 'we already have hired our woman guest conductor for the season.' But it does not bother me."

321   Feinman, Barbara. "The Women of the Clef: Female Composers on the Move." *Washington Post,* 3 April 1983, pp. C1, C8.

A lengthy article describing the founding of Leonarda Records, named after a gifted seventeenth-century Italian composer, Isabella Leonarda, who published over 200 works in 20 collections of her own. An excellent resource.

322   Gaume, M. M. "Ruth Crawford Seeger: Her Life and Works." Ph.D. dissertation, Indiana University, 1973.

323   Green, Mildred Denby. *Black Women Composers: A Genesis.* Boston: G. K. Hall & Co., 1983.

This informative and inspiring book is based on the author's 1975 D.Mus. dissertation at the University of Oklahoma, titled "A Study of the Lives and Works of Five Black Women Composers in America."

324   Gussow, Mel. "Elizabeth Swados Writes Cantata for Cabaret." *New York Times,* January 1977.

Twenty-five-year-old Elizabeth Swados, one of the most innovative composers in the American musical theater, is profiled in this article. She says in a memorable moment: "I would love to do a workshop with the New York Philharmonic to make them talk to their instruments, throw their instruments across the stage. They really need to loosen up."

325   Henahan, Donal. "Rebel Who Found a Cause." *New York Times,* November 1976, p. C21.

A summary of the environment in which Barbara Kolb, daughter of a jazz pianist, grew up and became a serious composer, is offered to the reader of this article.

326 Henahan, Donal. "She Steps In for Solti and Wins Ovation." *New York Times*, 2 November 1977, p. 23.

Margaret Hillis, the Chicago Symphony Orchestra's choral conductor for many years, steps in while in New York for an injured Sir George Solti and conducts the Eighth Symphony of Gustav Mahler. She conducted a triumphant performance and won a standing ovation from her audience, which from the start was supportive when the announcement was made that Sir George would not be able to conduct. This article describes the performance and the dynamics of the evening.

327 Henahan, Donal. "Training Grant for Conductors." *New York Times*, 17 May 1978, p. C17.

The announcement of a 3-million-dollar grant to the Juilliard School for the establishment of a long-range program for the development of young conductors is made in this article. The funds were given by Lila Acheson Wallace, a member of Juilliard's board of trustees and codirector of the Reader's Digest Association. Peter Mennin, the school's president, said, "I expect female candidates to audition and they will be welcomed." One wonders how many women have benefited from this remarkable and important program.

328 "Ina Ray Hutton, 67, Bandleader from the Mid-1930s to Mid-1950s, Dies." *Boston Globe*, 21 February 1984.

According to this obituary, Hutton conducted jazz orchestras from 1935 to the mid-1950s, using "sultry movements considered quite daring for that era." The early part of her career was spent leading an "all-girl orchestra," which was commercially successful for a time. The combination of sax and sex was taken to a large TV audience in the summer of 1956 when her musical variety show was broadcast by NBC.

329 Jezic, Diane Peacock. *Women Composers: A Lost Tradition Found.* New York: Feminist Press, 1988.

Jezic has written a guide to the lives and work of twenty-five composers of Western art music from the eleventh century to the present. The book makes music by women much more accessible and reveals a distinguished and courageous history.

330   Kerpferberg, Herbert. "Women of the Baton: The New Music Masters." *Parade Magazine,* 14 May 1978, pp. 4-5.

A summary of the recent work of Victoria Bond, Judith Somogi, Sarah Caldwell, and Antonia Brico. Brico was the real pioneer of the group, launching her career in the 1930s, and in response to the many difficulties she found, she formed an all women's orchestra. Excellent photographs included.

331   Kozian, Aldan. "Eve Queler Unearths the Offbeat." *New York Times,* 18 March 1984, pp. 21, 24.

Queler and her orchestra, functioning since 1971 as the Opera Orchestra of New York, specialize in concert performances of rarely heard operas. In this article she talks about why she became a conductor and how her ideas were always bigger than her technique could accommodate.

332   Lawson, Carol. "In SoHo, Revue of Songs by Women Tunesmiths." *New York Times,* 28 April 1978, p. C18.

About *Womansong,* a new musical revue at the Ward-Nasse Gallery in SoHo.

333   LePage, Jane Weiner. *Women Composers, Conductors, and Musicians of the Twentieth Century: Selected Biographies.* Vols. 1 and 2. Metuchen, N.J.: Scarecrow Press, 1980, 1983.

Thorough guides to the biographical details of thirty-four outstanding musical women, based on exhaustive personal interviews and documentary research. The biography of Sarah Caldwell included in this volume is particularly impressive.

334   Lieb, S. R. "The Message of Ma Rainey's Blues: A Biographical and Critical Study of America's First Woman Blues Singer." Ph.D. dissertation, Stanford University, 1976.

335 "Music of Louise Talma Presented." *New York Times,* 7 February 1977.
>A full concert of her music, presented at Hunter College, is reviewed.

336 Neuls-Bates, Carol. "Five Women Composers, 1587-1875." *Feminist Art Journal* 5 (1976): 32-35.

337 Neuls-Bates, Carol, Ed. *Women in Music: An Anthology of Source Readings from the Middle Ages to the Present.* New York: Harper & Row, 1982.
>An excellent book for use in music history teaching.

338 Page, Tim. "Gideon and Talma at 80 – Composers and Neighbors." *New York Times.*
>The long careers of composers Miriam Gideon and Louise Talma are discussed in this profile. Louise Talma has been a professor of music at Hunter College since 1952.

339 Pool, Jeannie G. *Women Composers of Classical Music: A Research Guide.* Boston: G. K. Hall & Co., 1982.
>Pool is also the author of *Handbook: Teaching the History of Women in Music* (Northridge, California State University, Department of Music, 1986). This 1982 book is for use in teaching as well.

340 Rockwell, John. "Ellen Zwilich Views Pulitzer as Double Win." *New York Times,* 4 May 1983, p. C17.
>As the first woman to win the Pulitzer Prize for music in its forty-year history, Zwilich comments, "I hope it is encouragement for other women. It's kind of a good sign for the world. We're not that far away from the days when orchestras resisted having women players. I'd like to think I won for my piece not as a symbol. But I don't mind being a positive symbol."

341 Rorem, Ned. "Woman: Artist or Artist-ess?" *Vogue* 155 (1 April 1970): 172;pl.

"Women have played a part (though small) in literature, the visual arts, and politics; but there have been no female composers."

342   Rosen, Judith, and Rabson, Grace Rubin. "Why Haven't Women Become Great Composers?" *High Fidelity* 23, no. 2 (February 1973): 46-53.
      A discussion of the many views on answers to the question. An excellent list of available recordings of works by women composers, to 1973, is included.

343   Skowronski, JoAnn. *Women in American Music: A Bibliography.* Metuchen, N.J.: Scarecrow Press, 1978.

344   Smith, G. Jean. "Dr. Brico Talks about Making Music." *National School Orchestra Association Bulletin,* February 1978, pp. 6-7.

345   Stern, Susan. *Women Composers: A Handbook.* Metuchen, N.J.: Scarecrow Press, 1978.

346   Tick, Judith. "Towards a History of American Women Composers before 1870." Ph.D. dissertation, City University of New York, 1979.

347   Tick, Judith. "Why Have There Been No Great Women Composers?" *International Musician* 79 (July 1975): 6, 22.

348   Vedder-Shults, Nancy, comp. *The Music of Women: A Selection Guide.* Madison: Wisconsin Women Library Workers, 1984.
      Basic record collection in five categories: concert music; jazz, blues; gospel; folk; and new women's music of feminist counterculture.

349 "Women Conductors." *Pan Pipes* 69 (1977): 4.

350 Zaimont, Judith Lang, et al., eds. *The Musical Woman: An International Perspective, 1983*. Vol. 1. Westport, Conn.: Greenwood Press, 1984.
       A landmark reference source in music history.

351 Zaimont, Judith Lang, et al., eds. *The Musical Woman: An International Perspective, 1984-1985*. Vol. 2. Westport, Conn.: Greenwood Press, 1987.
       A continuation of the powerful accomplishments of the first volume. Part 1 of this reference volume is entitled "Gazette" and documents recent news about women in music, including performances, prizes, discographies, festivals, and deaths of women composers. Nineteen essays on special topics of interest by noted scholars make up part 2 of this 557-page book.

352 Zaimont, Judith Lang, and Famera, Karen, eds. *Contemporary Concert Music by Women: A Directory of the Composers and Their Works*. Westport, Conn.: Greenwood Press, 1981.
       Thorough biographies and composition lists are given for seventy-eight living white American women composers in this directory.

Engineers

This is only a sampling of an extensive twenty-year literature well documented in other sources, such as Betty M. Vetter's article, "Women in Science and Engineering," which was published in *Women's Annual*, no. 5 (Boston: G. K. Hall & Co., 1985). Also, the Association for Women in Science maintains a national registry of women in scientific and engineering careers. More than 6,000 women in all areas of these fields are listed.

353 Berkwitt, G. "Weaker Sex Stars in Handling Heavy Parts: Simmons Co." *Mill and Factory* 73 (August 1963): 68-69.
       Discusses the recent legislation offering women equal pay and points out how much women are already doing at this bedding plant, including crane operation, because of the skill they display in judging distances and spotting loads.

354 "Charmglow Says Ladies Can Weld Too." *Welding Journal* 46 (December 1967): 1012.

A profile of a woman named Norma Brede who was a welder during the Korean War and who is now a welder in Wisconsin at a factory where outdoor gas lamps and gas-fired barbecues are made.

355 "Distaff Side to Ease Engineer Shortage." *Chemical Engineering* 70 (22 July 1963): 92.

356 D'Oro, P. J. "Women Who Make Cars." *Parade Magazine,* 15 December 1985, pp. 7-8.

About three women in the auto industry. Dr. Suzanne Gatchell holds a Ph.D. from the University of Michigan and is director of technical assessment, planning, and development for advanced vehicle engineering at General Motors in Pontiac, Michigan. Another, Marsha Sorace, service director for Paramus Honda in New Jersey, is boss to sixteen male mechanics. Finally, Jean Lindamood is executive editor of *Automobile* magazine. She was formerly an associate editor of *Car and Driver* magazine.

357 "Engineering Their Way to the Top." *Ebony* 40 (December 1984): 33-36.

An article about several black women engineers, outlining their struggles and successes throughout the country. The article mentions that only 5,000 black women are engineers in the United States. The profession's total number is 1,572,000.

358 Enterline, P. E. "Sick Absence for Men and Women by Marital Status." *Archives of Environmental Health* 8 (March 1964): 460-70.

Contains a bibliography in addition to the analysis. Discusses absentee rates of male and female engineers.

359 Feldman, S. "Increasing Role for Women in Electronic Engineering." *Electronic Industries* 23 (February 1964): 46-50.

360 "First International Conference of Women Engineers and Scientists, New York: June 15-21, 1964." *American Society for Heating, Refrigeration, and Air Conditioning Journal* 6 (August 1964): 44-45.

361 Forssman, S. "Women at Work: Health and Sociomedical Problems Related to the Employment of Women." *Industrial Medicine and Surgery* 33 (March 1964): 125-29.

362 "Gentlemen, We Are Joined." *Quality Progress* 1: (June 1968): 5-8.
A profile of Mae Goodwinn-Tarver, research statistician and internal quality-control consultant for Continental Can Company.

363 Glover, J. L. "Women and Engineering." *Electronics and Power* 14 (September 1968): 380.
A letter to the editor on the subject of attracting and using women in the engineering sciences.

364 Hamilton, J. L. "Should Your Daughter Be a Civil Engineer?" *Civil Engineering* 38 (August 1968): 96.

365 Holland, Ted. "Plenty of Room for Women Engineers." *Engineering* 207 (14 March 1969): 410.
A hopeful article in a British publication that closes with the idea that it would be good to look back at 1969 as the year women moved into engineering in more significant numbers.

366 Kleiman, Carol. "A Top-Paying Job? It Can Be Mechanical." *Chicago Tribune,* 16 September 1984.
About national trends in mechanical engineering, and specifically Kathleen M. Dages, a mechanical engineer at Commonwealth Edison in the cities of Dresden, Lasalle, and Zion.

367 Larange, M.N. "Where Working Women Stand Today." *Iron Age* 201 (20 June 1968): 68-69.

A discussion of a recent interview with Mary Dublin Keyserling, director of the U.S. Women's Bureau, about the "underuse of womanpower" in the United States.

368　"Leave It to the Girls (or the Saga of the Female Engineering Student)." *Mechanical Engineering* 90 (January 1968): 81.

About a course offered on Saturday afternoons to UCLA women engineering students in poise, make-up, and building self-confidence offered by the dean of women.

369　LeBold, William, project director. *Putting It All Together: A Model Program for Women Entering Engineering.* A special project sponsored by the Department of Freshman Engineering, Purdue University, West Lafayette, Ind., and the Women's Educational Equity Act (WEEA) Program, U.S. Dept. of Education. Newton, Mass.: WEEA Publishing Center, 1982.

A significant and extensive annotated bibliography strengthens an already strong project booklet from Purdue University's Department of Freshman Engineering. Much evidence of interest in recruiting women noted. For more information, contact the Education Development Center, 55 Chapel Street, Newton, MA 02160.

370　"Meeting on Women in Chemical Engineering: London, March 24." *Chemistry and Industry,* 29 March 1969, pp. 394-95.

371　"The Men Vote Her O-Kay: Girl on a Survey Crew." *California State Employee,* 12 August 1966, p. 9.

About Kay Griffin, a twenty-four-year-old junior civil engineer who became a full member of a preliminary survey team in April of 1966 in San Diego, California. After she completed this assignment, according to the article, she wanted to go into highway engineering, which is what interested her most. One of the earliest articles examined in the study leading to this book. It is based on the sexist notion that the men were men, but the woman in question was a girl.

372　"Nation's Leading Woman Civil Engineer, Elsie Eaves, Retires from ENR." *Engineering News* 170 (21 March 1983): 195-96.

373   Neal, Matty. "Technical Women." *Science and Technology,* September 1967, p. 13.
      The author, a mechanical engineer, comments on her experiences at the Second International Conference of Women Engineers and Scientists held in Cambridge, England.

374   *Options in Engineering: A Handbook for Entering Women Engineers.* Berkeley: University of California, Center for the Study, Education, and Advancement of Women, 1981, 38 pp.
      A career profile.

375   "Outstanding Engineer, Manager, and Consultant Is a Woman: Dr. Beatrice A. Hicks." *Product Engineering* 39 (8 April 1968): 137-38.

376   Peden, I. C. "New Faces of Eve: Women in Electrical Engineering." Bibliography. *IEEE Spectrum* 5 (April 1968): 81-84.

377   Popper, H. "Plant That Is Manned by Women." *Chemical Engineering* 72 (29 March 1965): 102;pl.

378   Popper, H. "What You Should Know about Women Engineers." *Chemical Engineering* 74 (11 September 1967): 165-72.

379   Rausch, H. "Engineers Call Her Boss." *Electronics* 39 (12 December 1966): 179-81.
      A profile of Rima Vasilyeva, chief of an electronic laboratory.

380   Roberts, G. "Wanted: Women Engineers and More Chance for Them." *Production Engineering* 39 (8 April 1968): 126-35.

381   Smyth, S. O. "Man's World? Not to These Women!" *Radio-Electronics* 38 (July 1967): 62.

382   Teltsch, Kathleen. "One of the Guys: The Engineer of Today Is Often a Woman." *New York Times,* 19 September 1985.

383   "U.S. Needs Women Engineers." *Mechanical Engineering* 85 (August 1963): 79-80.

384   Wheeless, Virginia Eman, and Stitzel, Judith G. "Meeting the Communications Needs of Women in Non-Traditional Occupations." In *Communication, Gender, and Sex Roles in Diverse Interaction Contexts,* edited by Lea P. Stewart and Stella Ting-Toomey. Communication and Information Science Series, edited by Melvin J. Voight. Norwood, N.J.: Ablex Publishers, 1986.
      About a study of the communication needs of women engineering students.

385   "Women Are Handy with MiG Guns." *Welding Engineer* 52 (November 1967): 53.

386   "Women Are Successful in Engineering Practice." *Automation* 14 (January 1967): 32.
      A report of a new study by Dr. William K. Lebold and Dr. Carolyn Perucci in which sixty-six women engineers were interviewed. They graduated in engineering from Purdue University between 1933 and 1964.

387   "Women Called to Engineering." *Chicago Tribune,* 14 June 1984.
      The president of Rensselaer Polytechnic Institute in Troy, New York, asserts that his solution to edging out the Japanese in engineering is womanpower.

388   "Women Can Wear Hard Hats Too." *Engineering* 171 (26 September 1963): 50.

389   "Women in Engineering." *Engineer* 228 (April 1969): 39.

390 "Young Women in Engineering." *Mechanical Engineering* 85 (March 1963): 56-57.

Scientists

391 Aldrich, Michele L. "Women in Science." *Signs* 4, no. 1 (1978): 126-35.
    Divided into the following sections: statistics on women in science; women and the history of science; women as students of science; and conferences and major studies on women in science. This review essay provides a thoughtful review of the literature of the time and some interesting comments on what is missing from it.

392 "Alumnae in the Sciences: How They Got There from Here." *Wells College Express* 5, no. 1 (May 1989): 13-24.
    A mathematician at the National Science Foundation, a chemist at the National Institute of Standards and Technology, an AIDS researcher at Walter Reed Army Medical Center, and an ecologist at North Carolina State University all discuss their scientific careers. With an introduction by Carroll Wetzel Wilkinson on issues scientists share with other women in nontraditional fields.

393 Bleier, Ruth. *Science and Gender.* New York: Pergamon Press, 1984.
    A provocative feminist monograph on the complexity of the scientist's work and the special pressures on her as a woman.

394 Campbell, David. "The Clash between Beautiful Women and Science." In *The Professional Women,* edited by A. Theodore. Cambridge, Mass.: Schenkman, 1971.
    The stereotype that only unattractive women work in male-intensive fields is discussed.

395 *Choices for Science: Proceedings of a Symposium Sponsored by the Mary Ingraham Bunting Institute of Radcliffe College.* Cambridge, Mass.: Harvard University Press, 1980, 60 pp.
    Contains papers by Jonathan R. Cole, Rhonda Hughes, Bonnie Spanier, Sonja M. McKinlay, Jill C. Bonner, and a panel on "Ethical

Choices for Science." This is a collection of papers, including: "Meritocracy and Marginality: Women in Science Today and Tomorrow" by Jonathan Cole; "Status of Women in the Physical Sciences, Mathematics, and Engineering" by Rhonda Hughes; "Critical Filters in Science Careers" by Bonnie Spanier; "Objectivity in Clinical Trials" by Sonja M. McKinlay; "The Cult of Objectivity in the Physical Sciences" by Jill C. Bonner. The Hughes, Bonner, and Spanier articles are particularly relevant to this study because of their considerations of the social dynamics women experience in these fields.

396　Cole, Jonathan R. *Fair Science: Women in the Scientific Community.* New York: Free Press, 1979.
　　　A provocative book taking up the question of whether the sciences are equitable for women or not.

397　Cress, Lois. "Chemist, Scholar, and Author: At 100, She Shuns Special Attention." *Denver Post,* 1 July 1977, p. 23.
　　　This article is a portrait of Mary Walsche, originally of Thurmont, Maryland, and now (in 1977) of Boulder, Colorado. She was an early graduate in 1906 of Purdue University with a B.S. in chemistry and a minor in mathematics, and she worked for a smelting firm in Catoctia, Maryland, as their chemist.

398　Ferry, Georgina. "WISE [Women in Science and Engineering] Campaign for Women Engineers." *New Scientist* 101 (January 1984): 10-11.

399　Haas, Violet B., and Perucci, Carolyn Cummings. *Women in Scientific and Engineering Professions.* Ann Arbor: University of Michigan Press, 1984.
　　　An authoritative reference source.

400　Hetrick, Haydée, et al. *A Profile of the Woman Engineer.* New York: Society of Women Engineers, 1984.
　　　The report is based on data obtained by surveying nonstudent members of the Society of Women Engineers 1983-84.

401 Kistiakowsky, Vera. "Women in Physics: Unnecessary, Injurious, and Out of Place?" *Physics Today*, February 1980, pp. 32-39.

The author establishes a brief history of women's contributions to international science and then she focuses on women physicists in the United States. She discusses trends and issues for women physicists as of 1980 and stresses the encouragement of women with interest, aspiration, and ability.

402 McDonald, Kim A. "Portrait: Sandra Faber, the Seven Samurai, and the Search for the Great Attractor." *Chronicle of Higher Education*, 21 September 1988, p. A3.

The article offers a biographical sketch of Dr. Sandra M. Faber, an astronomer on the faculty of the University of California at Santa Cruz. She identifies herself in the interview as a strong supporter of women in science, but she says she has not been a vocal advocate and has purposely avoided controversy.

403 Malcom, Shirley Maheley, et al. *The Double Bind: The Price of Being a Minority Woman in Science*. Washington, D.C.: American Association for the Advancement of Science, 1975.

A report of a conference of minority women scientists at Airlie House in Warrenton, Virginia. The precollegiate experience, professional education, career experience, the diversity of race and culture, and policy recommendations are discussed.

404 Mattfeld, Jacquelyn A., and Van Aken, Carol G., eds. *Women and the Scientific Professions: The MIT Symposium on American Women in Science and Engineering*. Cambridge, Mass.: MIT Press, 1965.

In October of 1964, the Association of Women Students at MIT sponsored a symposium that turned into an important conference about the problems of women in the scientific and engineering professions (260 students attended and there were 600 additional guests). The speakers included Jessie Bernard, Bruno Bettelheim, Richard H. Bolt, Mary I. Bunting, Erik Erickson, Lillian Gilbreth, Thomas W. Garrington, Jr., Alice Rossi, and many other intellectual and business leaders. These were the goals of the symposium: first, to acquaint women seriously interested in a career in science and/or technological fields with the mythical and actual difficulties ahead; second, to bring outstanding men and women together to discover new approaches and solutions to existing problems; and third, to attract favorable attention of industry, educational institutions, and the public at large to decrease the present barriers to women. This is a fascinating collection of addresses. Many of the issues raised in 1964 are still highly pertinent today.

405   National Research Council Committee on the Education and Employment of Women in Science and Engineering. *Climbing the Ladder: An Update on the Status of Doctoral Women Scientists and Engineers.* Washington, D.C.: National Academy Press, 1983.

406   Parker, Beulah. *Evolution of a Psychiatrist: Memoirs of a Woman Doctor.* New Haven: Yale University Press, 1987.

The author of *A Mingled Yarn* and *My Language Is Me* writes an autobiography in eight chapters. She begins with "Background," "The World That Was, 1912-1929," "The World between 1929 and 1939," "Becoming a Doctor, 1939-1953," "Emerging into the Field of Psychiatry," "Marriage," and continues with "Forty Years in Private Practice." A fascinating book throughout, but of particular relevance to this study is the section pp. 166-78. This contains her explication of being a woman in a "man's profession," in which she gives some insight into the dynamics she faced as a 1933 graduate of Bryn Mawr and as a doctor coming into her own during World War II.

407   *Programs in Science, Mathematics, and Engineering for Women in the United States, 1966-1978.* Washington, D.C.: American Association for the Advancement of Science, Free Project on Women in Science, 1978.

408   Ramaley, Judith A., ed. *Covert Discrimination and Women in the Sciences.* American Association for the Advancement of Science (AAAS) Selected Symposium no. 14. Boulder, Colo.: Westview Press, 1978.

Ramaley raises many important issues. 1) What behavior constitutes discrimination? 2) How is it defined operationally? 3) What federal and local programs have been implemented to remove discriminatory practices? 4) What factors other than obvious hiring and promotional practices can hinder women in their professional development? 5) What pressures operate to deflect women from scientific careers? 6) How can these problems be resolved so that more women will feel free to choose scientific careers? 7) What is the interplay between individuals and institutions in the process of promotion and tenure and other processes of professional advancement? 8) Are there differences in the ways that the performances of men and women are judged, and if so, how can this be changed?

409 Rossi, Alice. "Barriers to the Career Choice of Engineering, Medicine, or Science among American Women." In *Women and the Scientific Professions,* edited by J. Mattfeld et al. Cambridge, Mass.: MIT Press, 1965.
A thorough analysis of the issues in the mid-1960s.

410 Rossiter, Margaret W. *Women Scientists in America: Struggles and Strategies to 1940.* Baltimore: Johns Hopkins University Press, 1982.
She discusses territorial discrimination and hierarchical discrimination. A landmark study.

411 Searing, Susan E., ed. *The History of Women and Science, Health, and Technology: A Bibliographic Guide to the Professions and the Disciplines.* Madison: University of Wisconsin, Women's Studies Library, 1988.
A fifty-four-page annotated bibliography of materials on the history of women in science, health, and technology for use as a resource for curriculum development, professional reading, and student research. Done in collaboration with the Women's Caucus of the History of Science Society, this guide says, "The bibliography touches on many topics that have inspired feminist scholars for over a decade, including: women's experiences in the workplace; women's education for the professions; the interplay of scientific theory and social norms."

412 Siegel, P. J. *Women in the Scientific Search: An American Bio-Bibliography.* Metuchen, N.J.: Scarecrow Press, 1985.
An important reference book documenting the lives and writings of 150 women anthropologists, archeologists, psychologists, home economists, educators, and mathematicians.

413 Stitzel, Judith, and Wheeless, Virginia. "What Women in Science and Engineering Tell Us about Women's Studies." In "Science

Education and Feminist Education." *Women's Studies Quarterly* 11, no. 3 (Fall 1983): 23-24.

Overall, a discussion of the session at the National Women's Studies Association's annual meeting on science education and feminist education. Dr. Judith Stitzel of West Virginia University opened the session with a discussion of the paper she coauthored with Dr. Virginia Wheeless on "What Can Women in Science and Engineering Tell Us about Women's Studies?". (See entry 384.)

414   Whyte, J. *Girls into Science and Technology.* London: Routledge and Kegan Paul, 1986.

415   *Women and Science: A Special Issue. Resources for Feminist Research* 15, no. 3 (November 1986).

An introduction to issues and sources of information on them.

416   Zuckerman, H., and Cole, Jonathan R. "Women in American Science." *Minerva* 13, no. 1 (1975): 82.

A discussion of trends and issues for women in the sciences in the mid-1970s.

Surgeons

417   Davidson, L. R. "Sex Roles, Affect, and the Woman Physician: A Comparative Study of the Latent Social Identity upon the Role of Women and Men Professionals." Ph.D. dissertation, New York University, 1975.

418   Dowie, Mark. "Nancy Ascher, M.D.: On the Frontiers of Medicine." *Ms.,* November 1987, pp. 86-90.

A biographical portrait of surgeon Nancy Ascher, who is the clinical director of the liver transplant program at the University of Minnesota. She is a 1974 graduate of the University of Michigan Medical School and a person who was drawn to the intellectual challenge of surgery and the challenge of working with her hands. Her research involves xenografting—that is, transplanting organs from other species. Up until now, this medical specialization has been a very male world; "in fact the last true patriarchy in medicine where women are nurses, or transplant coordinators."

419 Hammond, J. M. "Women in Medical School: The Negotiation and Management of Status and Identity of Women in a Male-Dominated Institution." Ph.D. dissertation, Syracuse University, 1977.

420 Morgan, Elizabeth. *The Making of a Woman Surgeon.* New York: G. P. Putnam & Sons, 1980.
Morgan's first book is about her training as she worked to become a surgeon.

421 Morgan, Elizabeth. *Solo Practice: A Woman Surgeon's Story.* Boston: Little, Brown, 1982.
Not by any means a literary genius, Dr. Morgan tells her story, and she is quite full of herself. But the reader gets a sense of the pressures, the coping mechanisms, and the patient caseload of a plastic surgeon. Readers should bear in mind the highly publicized custody case regarding the author's daughter and form their own conclusions.

422 Nadelson, C. C. "Women in Surgery." *Archives of Surgery* 102 (March 1971): 234-35.

423 Shapiro, C. S. "A Woman in a Non-Traditional Role: Surgeon." *Educational Horizons* 53 (Spring 1975): 106-9.

424 Wilson, Dorothy Clarke. *Take My Hands: The Remarkable Story of Dr. Mary Verghese.* New York: McGraw-Hill, 1963.
A biography of a woman surgeon in India. She practiced in the Vellore Christian Medical College in South India, an institution that had been founded by Dr. Ina Scudder in the early part of the twentieth century. Half of the students were routinely women. The doctor was paralyzed from the waist down as the result of a bus accident. She

trained in part in the United States and was herself particularly dedicated to the surgical needs of the handicapped patient.

425 Wrenn, Marie-Claude. *You're the Only One Here Who Doesn't Look Like a Doctor: Portrait of a Woman Surgeon.* New York: Crowell, 1977.

A documentary of one year in the life of a woman surgeon shortly after she graduated from medical school. The author says: "Her tale is not written here as a universal or even feminist experience, but as a personal one peculiar to her and her times in an age where women are breaking unknown professional ground, in a society which is still ambivalent toward the professional woman, in a field where women are yet a small minority." As of 1975, 3.1 percent of the women in medicine in the United States had chosen to specialize in surgery. Insights into the macho world of surgery exist throughout the book.

Technological Fields

High-Technology Professionals

This literature documents, in part, one of the fastest-developing areas of employment options for women. The high-technology careers include telecommunications, robotics, space and air travel, and specialized areas of computer science and engineering, among others.

426 Bailyn, Lotte. "Experiencing Technical Work: A Comparison of Male and Female Engineers." *Human Relations* 40, no. 5 (1987): 299-312.

In 1985, Bailyn surveyed 279 women engineers and 155 men, and then found 51 pairs of responses that could be studied in depth regarding ways they each experienced technical work. She found that technically competent women feel ambivalent toward their technical expertise, especially when they are single. In trying to explain this finding, Bailyn asserts that the societal view of technical work is "gender alien" for women. But she thinks an explanation may also lie in the "way that organizations mandate the practice of technical work." She cites Evelyn Fox Keller's work as critical to making room in scientific fields for a diversity of approaches in the workplace.

427 Feingold, Norman, and Miller, Norma. *Emerging Careers: New Occupations for the Year 2000 and Beyond.* Garrett Park, Md.: Garrett Park Press, 1983.

428 Goldman, Sherli Evens. "Computers – and Liberated Women?" *Computers and People,* October 1974, pp. 8-10.

A brief assessment of where women stand in the computer industry as of 1974. Portraits of a woman who worked as a work-package manager at TRW Systems, a manager of employee communication for computer marketing, and a vice president of marketing are included in the article.

429 Haynes, H. Patricia. "Women Working: A Field Report." *Technology Review,* November-December 1984, pp. 37-38, 47.

Haynes traces her good beginnings in mathematics in Catholic women's schools and then the abrupt end to the era of encouragement when she began a master's degree in environmental engineering at a large public university where she encountered sex discrimination for the first time. She describes her work as a senior engineer for a hazardous-waste program of the Environmental Protection Agency (EPA), and some of the occupational difficulties she has experienced. She encourages the use of female role models. She also proposes some "rules of thumb" for employers and employees, both male and female. They include: 1) Search for the work of women in your field. 2) Know women's anger when you see it and do not equate it with bitchiness, defensiveness, or overemotionalism. Respect it. 3) For men: seek out women as colleagues and assume they have made important contributions in their fields. 4) For women: establish the independence and power of your own work. 5) Also for women: refuse anyone the power to deplete you of your passionate inquiry. Find and cherish its poetry.

430   Marrs, Texe W. *High-Technology Careers*. Homewood, Ill.: Dow Jones-Irwin, 1986.

The high-growth occupational fields of military engineering, telecommunications, robotics, space and air travel, computers, lasers, bioengineering, pharmaceuticals, medical technology, and advanced energy sources are discussed.

431   Turkle, Sherry. "Women and Computer Programming: A Different Approach." *Technology Review*, November-December 1984, pp. 48-50.

Turkle, author of *The Second Self: Computers and the Human Spirit*, discusses her research on children and computers. She has found that "some of the problems that girls experience in introductory programming have to do with the social construction of programming as male." She suggests that both hard mastery and soft mastery are appropriate to computer programming, thus blending qualities of the engineer and the artist. She says that "the computer connects the abstract to the physical, the sensual, and the psychological," and blending the two traits together in a gender-free computer world of the future is an important goal.

432   Wider Opportunities for Women (WOW). *Bridging the Skills Gap: Women and Jobs in a High-Tech World.* Washington, D.C.: WOW, 1983, 32 pp.

Lengthy bibliography and an issue brief on the question of changing technologies and changing jobs for women.

433   Zimmerman, Jan, ed. *The Technological Woman: Interfacing with Tomorrow.* New York: Praeger, 1983.

Past, present, and future roles of women in technology are discussed.

Pilots and Astronauts

It is unrealistic to plan future space flights without coming to grips with the problem of women. Naturally, the women would be fully operational crew members . . . not only there for sex.

—A NASA official, 1972

434   "Accolades Fly at Silver Wings Tribute to Women Pilots." *Chicago Tribune,* 26 June 1985.

The Illinois chapter of Silver Wings holds meeting to celebrate women pilots.

435   Agus, Carole. "Sally Ride: First of a New Breed." *Boston Globe,* 26 December 1982, p. A22.

A lengthy profile of Dr. Ride's qualifications and background. One of the most interesting points made is that she is not eligible for command because she is not a jet pilot. NASA created two astronaut classes: pilot astronauts and mission-specialist astronauts. Women can only become mission specialists at present. An interesting example of gender tracking in the American work force.

436   "American Woman Ready to Step Out into Space." *Chicago Tribune,* 11 October 1984.

Kathy Sullivan is preparing to become the first American woman to step into open space. As part of the *Challenger* crew she is to move the antenna, disconnected earlier, so that an in-cabin astronaut can throw a switch to drive two locking pins through.

437   Ball, Aimee Lee. "When Mom Is an Astronaut: Anna Fisher Will Become the First Mother in Space." *Parade,* 28 October 1984, pp. 4-7.
　　　About Kristen, age 1, and her astronaut parents, Anna and Bill.

438   Casselberry-Manuel, Diane. "Whirly Girls: Aloft for a Living." *Christian Science Monitor,* 6 April 1982, p. 22.
　　　About helicopter pilots who are women.

439   *"Challenger's* Happy Landing: The Space Shuttle Ends a Nearly Perfect Mission and Makes Sally Ride a Star." *Newsweek,* 4 July 1983, p. 68.
　　　Brief article about the successful return of the *Challenger* spacecraft in 1983. There were a few people at the California landing carrying posters that read: "A woman in space today, equality tomorrow."

440   Cipalla, Rita. "Sky's No Limit: It Was Love at First Sight for the Whirly Girls." *Chicago Tribune,* 29 March 1987, p. 8.
　　　About several members of the Whirly Girls, an organization begun in 1955 to provide a support network for women who flew helicopters. There are 570 members at present.

441   Dall'Acqua, Joyce. "High-Flying Women Sold the Public on Safety of Air Travel." *Tempo (Chicago Tribune* magazine), 31 March 1986, pp. 1-2.

442   David, Marjorie. "They Also Served: A Salute to the Women Who Manned the Lanes at Home." *Chicago Tribune,* 22 March 1987.
　　　A brief article about some women who served during World War II as WASPS (Women Airforce Service Pilots). They went through the same six months of training as the men training as pilots, yet they were classified as civil servants and did not qualify for veterans' benefits.

443   Fisher, James. "'This Is Really Great' Says Sullivan As She Takes a 17,000-MPH Spacewalk." *Boston Globe,* 12 October 1984, p. 6.

Dr. Kathryn Sullivan, the first American woman to walk in space, installed a line connecting two hydrazene full tanks and helped lock a faulty dish antenna during her workday in space, according to this article.

444   Goodman, Ellen. "Tribulations of a First Woman." *Boston Globe,* 23 June 1983, p. 19.

On Sally Ride's sixth day in space, Goodman discusses the extra responsibility for womankind that each first woman has to carry. (She also remarks that Ride's résumé makes Neil Armstrong look like an underachiever.)

445   Greene, Bob. "Oh, Bob: A Woman Wrote This Headline." *Chicago Tribune,* 28 October 1986.

About the author's nervous condition once he realized that the American Airline DC-10 he was flying on had a female first officer. In a follow-up article on 29 October 1986 he relates meeting the pilot, Ann Singer.

446   Interview with Emily Harrahan Howell, commercial airline pilot. In *Conversations: Working Women Talk about Doing a "Man's Job,"* edited by Terry Wetherby. Millbrae, Calif.: Les Femmes Press, 1977.

Howell discusses her satisfactions and dissatisfactions with the job. (See entry 131 for full annotation on book.)

447   Klemesrud, Judy. "Corporate World Is Hiring More Women as Pilots." *New York Times,* 1 January 1984.

An introduction to the lives of corporate pilots who are female.

448   Klemesrud, Judy. "Space: New Frontiers Opened to Women." *New York Times,* 29 June 1979, p. A16.

About the women who work as engineers and astronauts in the space centers around the country. At that time there were 439 women who were working in science and engineering professions at the seventeen NASA offices in the United States. Six of the thirty-five astronauts in training were women.

449　Lamb, Rosemarie Wittman. "Second Woman in Space Puts Her Career First." *Chicago Tribune,* 25 June 1984.

This article discusses Judith Resnik, the United States' second woman astronaut, including some of her early background in Akron, Ohio, and her later career with NASA.

450　Lehman, Betsy. "Yonder and Back–All-Women Crew on Medical Flight." *Boston Globe,* 17 May 1983.

About the culmination of months of planning by the United States Air Force to assemble a crew of three pilots, two flight engineers, and two loadmasters, all of whom were women. Their mission was to fly a Lockheed C141B *Starlifter* on a medical evacuation mission from McGuire Air Force Base in southern New Jersey to Rhein-Main Air Base in Frankfurt, West Germany, and back again.

451　Lipinski, Ann Marie. "The Woman Pilot Who Took Off in a Big Way." *Chicago Tribune,* 29 May 1984.

About Bonnie Tiburzi, a pilot for American Airlines since 1973. She was the country's first female pilot.

452　McCullough, Joan. "The Thirteen Who Were Left Behind." *Ms.,* September 1973, pp. 41-45.

This article traces the history of thirteen women who were chosen and who went through the initial Mercury Astronaut Candidate Testing Program "demonstrating exceptional suitability as space pilots." This program began in 1959. With the help of the famous woman pilot Jacqueline Cochran, twenty-five prestigious and capable American women pilots were chosen for the same battery of rigorous tests that were being given to men at the time. The tests are described in detail; the fact that women were being tested at all is revealed to have been a closely guarded secret in 1961. In spite of the fact that "in the opinion of the scientists evaluating the test results, the women were as capable and as suitable for space flight; in some ways more suitable," they were all suddenly dropped from consideration. In 1961 NASA canceled all further testing of women. In the last part of the article, the sexual discrimination that the women faced is discussed in detail. A NASA official is quoted in 1972 as saying, "It is unrealistic to plan future space flights without coming to grips with the problem of women. Naturally, the women would be fully operational crew members . . . not only there for sex."

453 McFarland, Holly. "Women Win Seat in the Cockpit." *Christian Science Monitor,* 10 May 1978, p. 2.

This article profiles two flight engineers for United Airlines, and it includes some basic statistics about the fifty female members of the Airline Pilots' Association. The text mentions that "some major U.S. carriers that have women pilots are (in 1978) American with 4, Braniff with 4, Continental with 6, Delta with 4, Eastern with 1, United with 5, and Western with 6." The article also mentions Jill E. Brown of Baltimore, the first black female to qualify as a major airline pilot.

454 Mann, Judy. "Dr. Ride's Ride." *Washington Post,* 24 June 1983.

A column discussing the pathetically long time it took the United States to allow a woman to take a space flight. The author recalls the congressional hearing in 1962 at which John Glenn testified. Glenn pointed out that "the men go off and fight the wars and fly the airplanes and come back and help design and test and build them. The fact that women are not in this field is a fact of our social order."

Mann is highly complimentary to Dr. Ride not only for handling her duties as an astronaut in an exemplary fashion but also for enduring the tribulations of being a "first woman." With consummate understatement Ride remarks of her experience: "It may be too bad that our society isn't further along and that this is such a big deal."

455 Miller, Margo. "They Reign Mainly in the Plane." *Boston Globe,* 19 January 1983.

Half the eight-pilot staff of Maine Air, a commuter line serving Bar Harbor and Portland, Maine, and Boston from Bangor, Maine, is composed of women. This article describes their work, their low pay, and their working conditions.

456 Oakes, Claudia M. *United States Women in Aviation, 1930-39.* Smithsonian Studies in Air and Science, no. 6. Ann Arbor: University of Michigan, Books on Demand.

The author is associate curator at the Smithsonian's National Air and Space Museum in Washington, D.C. The book tells the story of stunt pilot Bethe Lunk, air racer Phoebe Omlie, the famous Amelia Earhart, sound-barrier breaker Jacqueline Cochran, and other women pilots, whose goals included convincing people that flying was safe and that women were good pilots.

457   Okie, Susan. "NASA Appeal Gave a Physicist Wings." *Washington Post,* 9 May 1983, pp. 1, 8.
       A detailed biographical portrait of Sally Ride.

458   Reinhold, Robert. "Americans in Space: Women Are Ready." *New York Times,* 7 June 1983, pp. C1, C9.
       Discussion of NASA's readiness to send women into space. Women were ready a lot sooner than NASA, at least twenty-five years before by this author's calculations. See also Joan McCullough's article, "The Thirteen Who Were Left Behind," annotated here in entry 452.

459   Reinhold, Robert. "Behind Each Astronaut Stand the Other Women of NASA." *New York Times,* 28 August 1983.
       About the small but growing group of women gaining a foothold in the space program in technical and scientific jobs. Excellent statistics about the women who have paved the way are included.

460   Ride, Sally, and Okie, Susan. *To Space and Back.* New York: Lothrop, Lee & Shepard Books, 1986.

461   Robinson, Donald. "Trained as Combat Pilots: Should U.S. Women Kill?" *Parade Magazine,* 25 January 1981, pp. 7-8.
       A brief discussion of the attitude that women should only train and serve in the armed forces, not go into combat. This article is based on a month-long series of interviews with USAF women and other officials including female generals, air force captains, and their male colleagues.

462   Sanborn, Sara. "Sally Ride, Astronaut: The World Is Watching." *Ms.,* January 1983, pp. 45-52, 87.
       Sally Ride's landmark achievements are discussed from an international perspective.

463   Satchell, Michael. "Now Women Pilots Get Their Turn with the Airlines." *Parade Magazine,* 25 June 1978, pp. 4-5.

It is impossible to make an objective assessment of this article as it contains judgments and quotations such as the following: "I just wish she weren't so good-looking. I can foresee a situation in which an excellent pilot will just go to pieces when a good-looking gal like her gets next to him. It is a very intimate situation in the cockpit." And: "I don't believe women should be allowed to fly at the wrong time of the month. One thing we have to learn is how they react to stress during that time. We just don't know. Same thing with menopause." There's more: "At a time when employment barriers are being broken down between the sexes, the airline cockpit has, until now, been one of the last bastions of male supremacy. It's obvious from talking with many older pilots that they feel a woman's place on an airplane is back in the cabin serving in the traditional role of flight attendant." And, finally: "I suppose if we have to have women pilots it would be better to have unattractive ones in the cockpit. If we find out they can't cut it as pilots, then they should depart as gracefully as possible." Satchell interviewed sixteen women pilots for this article, but little of their thinking is included.

464   Sawyer, Kathy. "Study Urges Missions to Moon, Mars." *Washington Post,* 18 August 1987, pp. 1, 4, A13.

     A report about the contents of Sally Ride's eleven-month study of the United States space effort and recent failures. Ride's report, entitled: "Leadership and America's Future in Space" (see the National Technical Information Service for the full text of this report), was direct and candid in its assessment that the United States can no longer be the undisputed international leader in all space endeavors. The report was coolly received by NASA officials, and Ride announced her resignation from the agency in May of 1987. Already demonstrating her courage as the first American woman in space and her membership in the presidential commission that investigated the *Challenger* disaster, Ride exhibited further bravery as she challenged conventional wisdom of the NASA administration in this report.

465   Schmidt, William E. "Young Space Enthusiasts Crowd Alabama Camp." *New York Times,* 8 September 1985.

     About a summer camp for aspiring astronauts run by the state of Alabama as part of its Space and Rocket Center. About 3,100 boys and girls attend each summer in week-long sessions.

466   Sherr, Lynn. "Remembering Judy." *Ms.*, June 1986, pp. 56-58.
        Sherr recalls her own memories of Judith Resnik, the electrical engineer who died in the explosion of the *Challenger* on 28 January 1986. She then asks Resnik's female colleagues Sally Ride, Anna Fisher, Kathryn Sullivan, Rhea Seddon, and Shannon Lucid to reminisce about their late friend.

467   "Soaring on Wings." *New York Times,* 18 December 1981.
        About Janice L. Brown, the woman who made aviation history in 1980 by flying the first solar-powered airplane, the *Gossamer Penguin.* A former teacher, she is now flying another such plane, the *Solar Challenger,* in the Philadelphia area.

468   Stevens, William K. "Feminism Paved Astronauts' Way." *New York Times,* 2 May 1982.
        One year in advance of her historic flight into space, Sally Ride acknowledges that the women's movement cleared the way for her to take a seat in the *Challenger's* cockpit. She said, "Without the movement I would not be about to become the first and so far the only woman to fly in space, since the Soviet Union's Valentina Tereshkova did it in 1963."

469   Tiburzi, Bonnie. *Takeoff: The Story of America's First Woman Pilot for a Major Airline.* New York: Crown Publishers, 1984.
        A popular autobiography.

470   Weintraub, Bernard. "Women Will Pilot Planes in the Air Force: A Three-Year Training Program Ends, They'll Fly Tankers and Cargo but Not Combat Fighters." *New York Times,* 11 March 1979, p. 23.
        This article covers the Air Force's decision, after three years of trials, to assign women as pilots of big C-141 cargo planes on missions around the world and on jobs to refuel tankers for all tactical aircraft.

471   "Willing to Fly, Sally Ride Says." *New York Times,* 15 October 1986.
        About Ride's appearance on the NBC news program "Today," where she praised NASA's recovery efforts after the *Challenger* disaster, and she said she had changed her mind about never going into orbit again.

472 "Woman to Make Debut as a Pilot." *New York Times,* 12 January 1973.

This article announces the debut of Emily Howell, 33, the first American woman to fly with a scheduled American carrier. She had been hired by Frontier Airlines as a second officer to fly Boeing 737s.

Other Selected Nontraditional Fields

Jockeys and the Racing World

In 1968, Kathy Kusner, after waging a court battle in Maryland, won the right to become a race rider, thus enabling her to enter the elite circle of jockeys licensed to ride on the flat at major tracks where gambling is legal. A number of other women followed Miss Kusner's example, and the novelty of a racetrack having a woman jockey was, for a time, a box office attraction.

–From a *Current Biography* article (November 1976, pp. 383-85) on jockey Robyn Caroline Smith

From 1969 to the present, exceptional women have enjoyed visibility and success as jockeys, but this study has not revealed that the masculine world of horse racing is any more tolerant of women riders than before. This literature reveals that these women are still marginalized tokens in spite of their superior skills and athletic abilities, and that there are very few of them overall.

473 Barrett, Janet. "First Track for Karen." *Parade Magazine,* 28 June 1981, pp. 12-15.

Karen Rogers, age 18, is competing on the New York circuit as a jockey. She sees Robyn Smith as her role model, a woman who had 245 wins in twelve years.

474 Berke, Art, ed. *The Lincoln Library of Sports Champions.* Vols. 11-14. Columbus, Ohio: Sports Resources Co., 1974.

A set of books designed to encourage reading among elementary and secondary schoolchildren. Kathy Kustner and Robyn Smith are included as riding champions.

475   Cady, Steve. "To Joan O'Shea, the Race Is the Thing." *New York Times,* 22 November 1972.

Joan O'Shea, age 47, was a jockey at Aqueduct at the time of this article. Most of her experience as a jockey was gained in Canada; she became Ontario's first woman jockey by riding at Woodbine. She has also ridden at Hialeah and Blue Bonnets in Montreal.

476   Cady, Steve. "Women Stablehands Bring Change to Belmont's Barns." *New York Times,* 18 September 1976, pp. 21-22.

This article gives insight into the supposed inroads women had made at the time in racing's "feudalistic structure." Cady says, "Inspired by equal rights progress, the emergence of women jockeys and a shortage of dedicated stablehands, growing numbers of young women are finding fulfillment as grooms, hot-walkers, and exercise riders." Excellent photos included with article.

477   Dexter, Pete. "Battling for Her Place." *Sports Illustrated,* 23 February 1987, pp. 48-52.

She had ridden at Santa Anita, Longacres, and Bay Meadows on the West Coast. She was the first woman to win a riding championship at a major thoroughbred meeting with 179 wins in 1986. One of her fellow jockeys noted: "Forget that she is a girl. I could always pick out a girl in a race – even my own wife who was a jockey when I met her. I think maybe it is they way they sit. But I can't pick Vicky out. She looks as natural and relaxed as anybody out here. And she rides tight, she rides a fine line. She isn't going to give anybody breaks out on the track." Vicky Aragon is this woman's name and she is a celebrity in Seattle, Washington, where she was a frequent winner. She also became well known there because of a whipping incident with a jockey named Victor Mercado. She hit him twice during a race and received a three-week suspension as a result. In this article she describes her intuitive sense of horse behavior and how important she thinks that is to winning races. She says, "What makes you good is if you can take the second or third best horse and win." She is a risk taker and has great confidence in her own abilities. She has parents who always assumed she could do what she set out to do, whatever it was.

478   Farago, Bill. "One Woman's Winning Ways: Jockey Denise Bondrot." *Boston Globe Sports Plus,* 3 November 1978, pp. 4-5.

At twenty-six years old, Denise Bondrot was an acknowledged champion. Her first ride was in 1972 at Leckingham Park, and she had already accumulated over 500 rides when interviewed for this profile. She was riding at the time of this article at Suffolk on a regular basis.

479 "A First in Racing: A Woman Steward." *New York Times,* 17 October 1969.

Martha V. Oberlies has become the first woman steward (on 16 October 1969) in a former bastion of male exclusivity: the New York State Racing and Wagering Board.

480 Gemme, Leila Boyle. *The New Breed of Athlete.* New York: Pocket Books, 1975.

One of the two women included in this book is Kathy Kustner, Olympic equestrian. Her battle with the Maryland State Racing Commission to become the first woman jockey licensed to race on the flat track is discussed.

481 Haney, L. *The Lady Is a Jock.* New York: Dodd Mead & Co., 1973.

About female jockeys in U.S.

482 Heise, Kenan. "Trainer Mary Klim Dies at 82: Picked 1st Female Jockey." *Chicago Tribune,* 15 April 1988.

Heise reports on the death of a Chicago-area horse owner and trainer who selected Diane Crump to carry her colors in a race at Florida's Hialeah Park in 1969. The article reports that she gave Crump the opportunity to be the first female jockey in February 1969. Male jockeys opposed this action because although the "girls" were capable as exercise riders, they claimed they were not strong enough and would endanger the lives of those who practice one of the world's most dangerous professions. According to this report, Klim countered with the following retort: "Crump is a smooth rider. She's cool enough and has enough gray matter to be as good a rider as any boy."

483 Hollander, Phyllis. *One Hundred Greatest Women in Sports.* New York: Grosset & Dunlap, 1976.

The author briefly discusses the new area of sport women recently have integrated: horse racing. "In 1968 Kathy Kustner of the

United States became the first licensed female jockey in the country. It was an important step denoting a slow but growing acceptance of women jockeys as important competitors in the world of horse racing."

484   "Jockey Was a Lady." *Sports Illustrated,* 5 July 1971, pp. 24-29.
    Picture story on women who work with horses and several who ride thoroughbreds as jockeys.

485   Katz, Michael. "A Woman Trainer Finds There's Room at the Top." *New York Times,* 16 June 1977.
    Top trainer Mary Cotter is profiled while working at Belmont Park.

486   Kisner, Ronald E. "Teen-Aged Girl Cracks Barrier on the Racetrack." *Jet,* 29 July 1971, pp. 46-49.
    This is a profile of a young black woman named Cheryl White who at the age of 17 was trying to become licensed as a jockey at Thistledown Racetrack in Cleveland, Ohio. She had also at the time been accepted at Bowling Green State University where she wanted to specialize in mathematics. One has to wonder what happened to this brave pioneer. The article is full of excellent photographs. She is quoted in the article as saying, "I'm going to be a jockey, not a jockette. That's some term the media dreamed up."

487   Maranto, Gina. "A Woman of Substance: Jockey Julie Krone 4' 10½" Looms Large at Monmouth." *Sports Illustrated,* 24 August 1987, p. 62.
    Krone won $2,357,156 in purses in 1986. This made her the number one female rider in the nation. She is from Eau Claire, Michigan, has a mother who is a horsewoman, and has ridden at Churchill Downs, Pimlico, and Bowie Racecourse in addition to Monmouth.

488   Naughton, Jim. "Karen Rogers's Spirit Remains Unbroken." *New York Times,* 30 June 1980.
    This story covers Karen Rogers's accident in a race at Monmouth Park. She took a bad fall that resulted in three fractured vertebrae. She was the country's leading female jockey at the time.

489   O'Neill, Lois Decker, ed. *The Women's Book of World Records and Achievements.* Garden City, N.Y.: Doubleday, Anchor Press, 1979.
        Especially useful for its recognition of women in sports in general and racing in particular. For example: "The United States' top jockey, male or female, in 1972 was Robyn Smith. She began a career in thoroughbred racing in 1969. In 1972 she finished 7th in international jockey standings with 98 mounts and a 20 percent winning percentage that could be bettered by only one jockey. All the others were European, so she was the best in the U.S."

490   Ramsden, Caroline. *Ladies in Racing, Sixteenth Century to the Present Day.* London: Stanley Paul & Co., 1973.
        According to Mary L. Remley, author of *Women in Sport: A Guide to Information Sources* (Detroit: Gale, 1980): "Chapters briefly review British women's involvement in horse racing including as owners, trainers, bookmakers, racing journalists, and jockeys. Emphasis is placed on horsewomen of the twentieth century."

491   "Robyn Caroline Smith." *Current Biography,* November 1976, pp. 383-85.
        A lengthy biography. Describes the mysterious nature of this woman's real identity and constructs as much verifiable detail as possible. This biography was written before Smith's marriage to Fred Astaire.

492   Ryan, Joan. *Contributions of Women: Sports.* Minneapolis: Dillon Press, 1975.
        Kathy Kustner's biography is included.

493   Stambler, Irwin. *Women in Sports.* Garden City, N.Y.: Doubleday & Co., 1975.
        Robyn Smith's accomplishments in horse racing are discussed.

494   "Two Pros." *Time,* 20 March 1972, pp. 103-4.
        Discusses contributions by tennis pro Billie Jean King and jockey Robyn Smith to the success of women in athletics.

495   "Woman Farrier Makes Union Debut at Race Track." *CLA Times*, 1979.

Ada Gates grew up around horses, and she has become the only female horseshoer in the United States and Canada with a union card. She works the southern California racetrack circuit and shoes horses at the Flintridge Riding Club near Pasadena. Her grandfather was a member of the New York State Racing Commission and started her riding at the age of four.

496   Young, O'Brien. "Vicky Aragon." *Women's Sports and Fitness* 9 (June 1987): 54.

A brief article about the nation's number four apprentice jockey, who says about herself, "On a horse, I'm a rider – not a man or a woman, but a rider." The author predicts that if she keeps winning she might ride her way to the Kentucky Derby. Another memorable quote: "I like everything about horses: their innocence, their cockiness, their energy. That's where I get my energy from, on the track or off."

Rabbis

I loved my little yeshiva. I loved what I learned there. And I have no memory at all – try as I might to resurrect one – of ever feeling the least bit put upon by any of its baleful medievalism. Sometimes I worry that I have become a rabbi not as an act of love, but of revenge. To redeem myself, not only from the religious mentors of my childhood, but from that happy moron – me. Nothing really bothered me in those days, and that bothers me now. I know I was just a child, steeped in the essence of childhood that Dylan Thomas called "once below a time." I was also in that state of preconscious, before-the-apple naïveté with which feminists are wincingly familiar.

– Rabbi Susan Schnur,
"Hers" column, *New York Times*, 18 July 1985

This review gives evidence of real progress for women in their entry into positions of religious authority and in their outreach to the women of their synagogues, especially during the last ten years. Although resistance is also a real factor, there is evidence of flexibility in some congregations and on the part of women themselves. The voices of the rabbis are heard in this literature, and there is evidence of both denial of gender as an important factor as well as expression of determination to continue to expand the boundaries for women in Judaism.

497 Austin, Charles. "Conservative Rabbis Rule Out Admission of a Woman to Group." *New York Times*, 13 April 1983, pp. 1, A23.

Rabbi Beverly Magidson's application for admission to the Rabbinical Assembly, the national organization for Conservative rabbis, was turned down. The article discusses the context of the decision.

498 Blechman, Barbara. "Rabbi Mindy Portnoy Talks to Barbara Blechman: A Woman Rabbi Is up against Centuries of Tradition." *Washington Post*, 23 October 1983, p. C3.

499 Cantor, Aviva. "Rabbi Eilberg." *Ms.*, December 1985, pp. 45-46.

About Conservative Judaism's first woman rabbi.

500 Cummings, Judith. "Woman Is in New Post as Conservative Rabbi." *New York Times*, 3 August 1986.

Rabbi Leslie Alexander works as assistant rabbi at the Congregation Adat Ari El in Los Angeles. She is the first woman to serve as a rabbi at a major Conservative Jewish congregation. According to this 1986 article, there are now 130 women in the United States who are rabbis.

501 Duncan, George. "Female Rabbinical Student Asks Increased Femininity in Judaism." *New York Times*, 7 May 1972.

"There is an urgent need to balance the predominantly masculine perspective in Judaism with a feminine counterpart, especially in regard to religious ceremonies, liturgy, and the creative arts. Among her suggestions for liturgical modifications she urged changes in the marriage ceremony that would create a mutuality of obligation rather than the one-sided sense of man's ownership of women and the double standard it implies." Sandy Eisenberg Sasso made these remarks to the American Jewish Committee at its sixty-sixth annual convention at the American Hotel. She is a rabbinical student at the Reconstructionist Rabbinical College in Philadelphia.

502 Franklin, James L. "Conservative Women Rabbis Predicted by 1985." *Boston Globe*, 18 April 1980.

A committee has been considering the issue since 1977.

503   Goldman, Ari L. "A Woman Finds Bias as a Rabbi." *New York Times,* 22 June 1984.
        A woman is the new rabbi at the Beth Shalom congregation in Clifton Park, New York. She is a Conservative Jew, who was ordained in the Reform seminary because as a woman, she could not gain admission at that time to the Conservative seminary.

504   Greenberg, Julie. "The Education of a Lady Rabbi." *Washington Post,* 2 July 1989, p. C5.
        The author became a rabbi on 18 June 1989 after six years of study at the Reconstructionist Rabbinical College of Philadelphia. She describes the real tensions between men and women in the school, but overall she expresses a deep sense of optimism about steady progress, growing acceptance of women in positions of religious authority, and the sense that she has an important part to play in shaping history as she accepts her first rabbinical job.

505   Haddad, Yvonne Y., and Findly, Ellison Banks. *Women, Religion, and Social Change.* Albany: State University of New York Press, 1985.
        Contains an article entitled "The Separation of Rabbinic Judaism," by Judith Baskin.

506   Herschel, Susannah, ed. *On Being a Jewish Feminist.* New York: Schocken Books, 1983.
        Contains Laura Geller's "Reactions to a Woman Rabbi."

507   Jensen, Cheryl. "First Woman Rabbi–10 Years Later." *Ms.,* February 1982, p. 20.

508   Kaiser, Robert Blair. "Drive Pressed for Ordaining Female Rabbis." *New York Times,* 23 March 1980, p. 40.
        About a demonstration on the steps of the Jewish Theological Seminary in New York City in favor of the ordination of rabbis for Conservative synagogues.

509 Kaiser, Robert Blair. "A Vote by Conservative Rabbis Backs the Ordination of Women." *New York Times,* 18 May 1980.
  A vote at the Rabbinical Assembly 156 to 115 favored ordination of women.

510 Mirsky, Norman. *Unorthodox Judaism.* Columbus: Ohio State University Press, 1978.
  Contains an article entitled "Pries and Prejudice," referring to the first woman rabbi, Sally Priesand.

511 "Ordination of Women as Rabbis Is Endorsed." *New York Times,* 18 November 1980.
  The Women's League for Conservative Judaism has called for the Conservative branch of Judaism to ordain women as rabbis.

512 Priesand, Rabbi Sally. *Judaism and the New Woman.* Introduction by Bess Myerson. Jewish Concepts and Issues Series. New York: Behrman House, 1975.
  Rabbi Priesand divides her book into the following sections: 1) "The Biblical Concept of Womanhood"; 2) "Rabbinic Attitudes toward Women"; 3) "Emancipation Brings Change"; 4) "Creation of the State of Israel"; 5) "Ritual"; 6) "Economic and Cultural Contributions of Women"; 7) "The Jewish Mother Stereotype"; 8) "Great Jewish Women"; and 9) "Creating Tomorrow's Jewish Woman." Rabbi Priesand shares her view of her religion and its need to accept modern women's needs. She includes a list of recommended readings and a glossary of terms. Of particular interest is her elaboration called "More Than Token Equality." She addresses women's rights as human beings, and she issues a challenge to Jewish women. She says they must take the lead in "coming to terms with the developments of the last century." She says women must sit down with individual rabbis and boards of trustees and demand the right to be involved in every aspect of the synagogue and the Jewish community.

513 "Rabbinical Students Marry." *Newark Star Ledger,* 26 June 1970.
  Sandra Eisenberg and Dennis Sasso, both students at the Reconstructionist Rabbinical College in Philadelphia, were married on 25 June 1970. The article speculates that when she graduates in four

years, "Sandra could be the first female rabbi in 4,000 years of Jewish history."

514   Rabinovitz, Barbara. "The Goal of Sheila May Cline: A Lovely Cantor She Would Be." *Boston Sunday Herald Traveler,* 7 March 1971.
       Recently accepted to the Union College School of Sacred Music in New York City, Sheila Cline wants to become a musical leader of a synagogue congregation.

515   Schnur, Susan. "Becoming a Rabbi: An Act of Love and Maybe of Revenge." *New York Times,* 18 July 1985.
       Rabbi Schnur writes the "Hers" column here and for several weeks after this one. This column concerns her memories of her education in a "little yeshiva" in Trenton, New Jersey, where the boys studied the Talmud and the girls went downstairs and made tuna-fish sandwiches.

516   Sendor, Liz Dowling. "Rabbi: Her Sex No Hindrance on the Maryland Campus. She Is Jewish Mother and Religious Teacher." *Boston Globe,* 14 October 1980, p. 2.
       About Rabbi Jan Kaufman of the University of Maryland's Hillel Foundation. "I don't talk about being a female rabbi," she says in a rapid-fire manner. "There's not one iota of difference between what I do and what my male colleagues do. In my job, being a woman is irrelevant." Nevertheless, some students belonging to the Orthodox branch of Judaism, which disapproves of women being ordained as rabbis, treat Kaufman as a joke. "They have a lot of contempt. They mock me. But I'm not sure whether they do it because I'm non-Orthodox, or because I'm a woman." Such incidents can hurt badly, Kaufman admits in this article, but she finds she must ignore the criticism. If she argued back, "that's all I would do. It would make me crazy." "I feel I have more to give to the Jewish community than my gender," she says at the close of this interview.

517   "Toppling a Jewish Tradition: A Conservative Seminary Votes to Ordain Women Rabbis." *Time,* November 1983, p. 48.

518 Vecsey, George. "Conservative Jewry to Vote the Ordaining of Women." *New York Times,* 13 January 1979, p. 23.

519 Vecsey, George. "Her Ambition Is to Become a Rabbi: And a Housewife." *New York Times,* 13 April 1971.
    On 3 June 1972 Sally Priesand will be ordained from the Hebrew Union College Jewish Institute of Religion, thus becoming the first woman rabbi in the history of Judaism.

520 "Women Clergy Identify with Workforce Counterparts." *Chicago Tribune,* 23 December 1986.
    This article discusses the findings of a survey conducted by the United Church of Christ's Coordinating Center for Women in Church and Society. The survey found that 60 percent of the women clergy responding (including rabbis) said they were rejected for a job because of their gender. Many also responded that they experience sexual harassment on the job and that they are paid less than men.

Police

521 "Career on the Force Began with an Impulse." *Chicago Tribune,* 4 June 1984.
    This is about Anne Egan, a twenty-eight-year-old woman who became a police officer in 1980. She currently works for the mounted police unit in Chicago, Illinois.

522 "Evanston Agrees to Hire 4 More Women as Police." *Chicago Tribune,* 24 August 1984.
    After being sued for discrimination, the city of Evanston is hiring more women into its police force.

523 "Fears about Job Give Way to Enthusiasm." *Chicago Tribune,* 4 June 1984.
    A profile of a woman whose nine years on the Chicago police force have included being the first woman to join the department's canine unit.

524   Gross, Jane. "More Female Agents in War on Drugs." *New York Times,* 16 February 1986.

About Joan T. Marin, a forty-two-year-old narcotics agent for the Federal Drug Enforcement Administration from Houston, Texas, who now works in Manhattan. Article mentions that nationwide there are 183 female agents in the agency's total work force of 2,422 (8 percent).

525   Jurik, Nancy R., and Halemba, Gregory J., eds. "Gender, Working Conditions, and the Job Satisfaction of Women in a Nontraditional Occupation: Female Correctional Officers in Men's Prisons." *Sociological Quarterly* 25 (August 1984): 551-66.

An exploratory analysis of the work orientations and job satisfaction levels of female correctional security officers compared to those of male officers working in the same institutions.

526   Martin, Susan Erlich. *Breaking and Entering: Policemen on Patrol.* Berkeley: University of California Press, 1980.

527   O'Brien, John. "For Thirty-Seven Years, an Anonymous Job: The Private Detective's Race Was Her Advantage." *Chicago Tribune,* 7 November 1984, p. 7.

A profile of the sixty-eight-year-old black private detective Caroline Kelley Ward, whose first job after college was working undercover for the War Department's Air Service Command watching for sabotage.

528   Quindler, Anna. "The Good Guys Aren't Always Guys." *New York Times,* 3 April 1986, p. 18.

A profile of Kathy Burke, a police detective who became a police officer eighteen years ago. Now there are 2,300 women on the force in New York.

529   Reardon, Patrick. "Ten Years Later, Women Cops Like Their Beat Just Fine." *Chicago Tribune,* 4 June 1984.

Fourteen policewomen joined the force in Chicago in 1974, and now there are 747. This article outlines their achievements and their views of their work.

530 Recktenwald, William. "One in Five Hopefuls Get into Police Training." *Chicago Tribune,* 12 November 1986.
Discusses attrition rates among police recruits.

531 "Sergeant Has Her Eye on Lieutenant's Spot." *Chicago Tribune,* 4 June 1984.
The first black Chicago police sergeant discusses how she is looking to the day of her next promotion.

532 Turner, Wallace. "Woman Quits as Portland Police Chief." *New York Times,* 3 June 1986.
Penny E. Harrington, the only female police chief in a major American city, resigned her job in Portland, Oregon. This article tells part of the story and leaves many questions unanswered about her brief seventeen months as chief.

533 "Women to Join Mexico State's Transit Police." *Chicago Tribune,* 13 September 1985.
Thirty-six women have been appointed to join the state transit police force in Morleos, Mexico, and eventually all transit police (300) will be replaced with women. Author's note: Researchers are urged to comment on this move.

534 "Women's Police Group Calls First Meeting." *Chicago Tribune,* 24 December 1985.
A brief article announcing the first meeting of the Illinois Women in Law Enforcement. The group is open to municipal, county, state, federal, and military female police officers.

Farmers

Though this is a literature of marginalization, loneliness, and isolation, it documents some individual progress as well. The recent scholarly studies, particularly by Sachs and Rosenfeld mark a new beginning in the recognition of the contributions and tribulations of women in authority on American farms.

535   Banas, Casey. "New Agricultural High School Sprouts on Chicago's Last Farm." *Chicago Tribune* 18 August 1985.

About the opening of the new Chicago High School for the Agricultural Sciences. It is the nation's second agricultural high school, and more than half the students in the first class will be female. The other agricultural high school is located in Philadelphia and is the Walter Biddle Saul High School of Agriculture.

536   Bentley, Susan, and Sachs, Carolyn E.. *Farm Women in the United States: An Updated Literature Review and Annotated Bibliography.* University Park: Pennsylvania State University, Department of Agricultural Economics and Rural Sociology, Agricultural Experiment Station, Center for Rural Women, 1984.

537   Bokemeier, Janet L., Sachs, Carolyn E., and Keith, Verna. "Labor Force Participation of Metropolitan, Nonmetropolitan, and Farm Women: A Comparative Study." *Rural Sociology* 48 (1983): 515-39.

538   Bokemeier, Janet L., and Garkovich, Lorraine. "Assessing the Influence of Farm Women's Self-Identity on Task Allocation and Decision Making." *Rural Sociology* 52, no. 11 (1987): 13-36.

The authors studied 880 Kentucky farm women in a statewide mail survey. They found some evidence of women's participation in egalitarian and conjoint decision making on farms. But, overall, the women did not report a high level of involvement in farm decisions. The article, in addition to reporting on an important study, cites many other works on farm women that are of substantial interest.

539   Boulding, Elise. "The Labor of U.S. Farm Women: A Knowledge Gap." *Sociology of Work and Occupations* 7 (1980):261-90.

540   Cebotarew, N., Blacklock, W., and McIsaac, L. "Farm Women's Work Patterns." *Atlantis: A Women's Studies Journal* 11, no. 2 (Spring 1986): 1-22.

541   Conway, Chris. "Farm Harvest: New Role of Women." *Chicago Tribune,* 30 January 1985.
         An extensive article covering the changing status of the farm women. Mentions that in the 1978 Census of Agriculture, farm operators were identified for the first time by sex. About 112,799 of the 2.47 million farms in the United States were listed as being operated by women. In 1982 the number increased to 121,599 of 2.24 million American farms.

542   DiPerna, Paula. "Up on the Farm." *Working Women* 4 (February 1979): 36-42.
         DiPerna outlines the new achievements of women in all aspects and roles of agriculture.

543   Elbert, Sarah. "Amber Waves of Gain: Women's Work in New York Farm Families." In *To Toil the Livelong Day: America's Women at Work: 1780-1980,* edited by Carol Groneman and Mary Beth Norton. Ithaca, N.Y.: Cornell University Press, 1987.
         Research on the farm women of New York State is discussed.

544   Fiske, Jo Ann. "Ask My Wife: A Feminist Interpretation of Fieldwork Where the Women Are Strong but the Men Are Tough." *Atlantis: A Women's Studies Journal* 11, no. 2 (Spring 1986): 59-69.

545   Flora, Cornelia Butler, and Johnson, Sue. "Discarding the Distaff: New Roles for Rural Women." In *Rural U.S.A.: Persistence and Change,* edited by Thomas R. Ford. Ames: Iowa State University Press, 1977.

546   Fowler, Becky. *Rural Women: An Annotated Bibliography, 1976-1979.*
      Morgantown: West Virginia University School of Social Work, 1979.
      The focus is on Appalachian women.

547   Geisler, Charles C., Walters, William F., and Eadie, Katrina L. "The
      Changing Structure of Female Agricultural Land Ownership
      between 1940 and 1978." *Rural Sociology* 50 (1985): 74-87.
          The authors conclude that the equalization of ownership
      between men and women has not yet balanced out, as family farms in
      America are patriarchal institutions. More research on women as
      owners of farmland is called for by the authors.

548   Graff, Linda L. "Industrialization of Agriculture: Implications for
      the Position of Farm Women." *Women in Agriculture and Rural
      Society,* special issue of *Resources for Feminist Research* 11 (1982):
      10-11.

549   Hagood, Margaret Jarman. *Mothers of the South: Portraiture of the
      White Tenant Farm Woman.* New York: W. W. Norton, 1977.
          Sachs comments in *The Invisible Farmers* (see entry 567) that
      this is an excellent study of tenant farm women of the 1930s. Hagood
      tried to give substance and meaning to statistical descriptions and she
      avoided the superficial, stereotyped, sentimental "case study" to give a
      richer sort of description than qualitative measures can give.

550   Hill, Frances. "Farm Women: Challenge to Scholarship." *Rural
      Sociologist* 1 (1981): 370-82.

551   Jensen, Joan. *With These Hands: Women Working on the Land.* Old
      Westbury, N.Y.: Feminist Press, 1981.
          A feminist perspective on farm women's history.

552   Jones, Calvin, and Rosenfeld, Rachel Ann. *American Farm Women:
      Findings from a National Survey.* National Opinion Research Center
      (NORC) Report no. 130. Chicago: NORC, 1981.

553 Joyce, Lynda M., and Leadley, Samuel M. *An Assessment of Research Needs of Women in the Rural United States: Literature Review and Annotated Bibliography.* Agricultural Economics and Rural Sociology Paper no. 127. University Park: Pennsylvania State University, Department of Agricultural Economics and Rural Sociology, Agricultural Experiment Station, 1977.

The authors conclude that little attention has been paid to the woman as an agricultural producer or as a partner in production.

554 Kalbacher, Judith Z. "Women Farmers in America." Paper no. ERS-679. Washington, D.C.: United States Department of Agriculture, Economic Research Service, 1982.

555 Kalbacher, Judith Z. "Women Farm Operators." *Family Economics Review* 4 (1983): 17-22.

Kalbacher, a geographer with the Economic Research Service, reports a significant increase in the number of farms operated or managed by women.

556 Knickerbocker, Brad. "Women Digging In on the Farm." *Christian Science Monitor,* 10 December 1979, p. 2.

Coverage of a seminar at the University of California at Davis on women in agriculture and some of the information exchanged there regarding women as farmers.

557 "More Women Crop Up at Farm Schools." *Chicago Tribune,* 25 August 1985.

Various administrative officials from Penn State, University of Vermont, and Purdue comment on the rising enrollment of women in their agricultural education programs.

558 Orr, Richard. "Farm Wives Taking to the Field with Men." *Chicago Tribune,* 28 October 1978, sec. 1, p. 10.

559 Pearson, Jessica. "Note on Female Farmers." *Rural Sociology* 44, no. 1 (1979): 189-200.

The author discusses her qualitative sociological research with eleven women in farming in southeastern Colorado.

560   Pearson, Jessica. "Women Who Farm: A Preliminary Portrait." *Sex Roles* 6 (1980): 561-74.

At the time of the article 483,000 women in the United States were employed in agriculture. Eleven indepth interviews were conducted with women in Baca County Colorado. The interviewees discussed satisfaction with "men's work."

561   Rosenfeld, Rachel Ann. *Farm Women: Work, Farm, and Family in the United States.* Institute for Research in Social Science Monograph Series. Chapel Hill: University of North Carolina Press, 1985.

Before writing this book the author oversaw, as principal investigator, a national survey of farm women for the U.S. Department of Agriculture. Her book in turn is the first about farm women in the United States that uses data from a national sample. Rosenfeld organizes her book into the following chapters: "Women, Work and Farming"; "The 1980 Farm Women's Survey"; "Farm and Home Work"; "Farm and Household Decision Making"; "Off Farm Employment"; "Community and Farm Voluntary Organizations and Political Bodies"; "Self-Perceptions of Farm Women"; and "The Study of Farm Women." She presents her findings with care and sensitivity in order to clarify what women on farms do and how they feel about it. She considers the paid and unpaid work of women, and uses discussions of their self-perceptions to elucidate their contributions. She establishes a clear context of the farm as an atypical workplace in this important book. Rosenfeld's bibliography is impressive and informative.

562   Rosenfeld, Stuart A., ed. *Brake Shoes, Backhoes, and Balance Sheets: The Changing Vocational Education of Rural Women.* Washington, D.C.: Rural American Women, 1981.

563   Ross, Peggy Johnston. *Farm Women's Participation in United States Agricultural Production: Selected Assessments.* Ph.D. dissertation, Ohio State University, 1982.

564   Rubenstein, Gwen. "Leading America's Cattlemen." *Leadership*, 1986.

About the first woman president of the National Cattlemen's Association. She lobbies for farm legislation.

565   Sachs, Carolyn E. "American Farm Women." In *Women and Work*, vol. 7, edited by Ann H. Stromberg, Laurie Larwood, and Barbara Gutek. Beverly Hills, Calif.: Sage Publications, 1987.

The chapter describes the various kinds of work farm women do now and have done in the past in the United States. Sachs explores why women have remained invisible farmers throughout agricultural history.

566   Sachs, Carolyn E. *The Displacement of Women from Agricultural Production: The Case of the United States*. Ph.D. dissertation, University of Kentucky, 1981.

567   Sachs, Carolyn E. *The Invisible Farmers: Women in Agricultural Production*. Totowa, N.J.: Rowman & Allanhed, 1983.

Based on her dissertation at the University of Kentucky, this monograph explores the strong societal tendency to see men as farmers and women as farmer's wives. Sachs explored women's contributions to agricultural production and really tried to analyze them without bias. Chapter 4 introduces readers to women farmers, who they are and why they farm.

568   Salamon, Sonja, and Keim, Ann Mackey. "Land Ownership and Women's Power in a Midwestern Farming Community." *Journal of Marriage and the Family* 41 (1979): 109-119.

569   Scholl, Kathleen K. "Classification of Women as Farmers: Economic Implications." *Family Economics Review*, no. 4 (1983): 8-17.

570 "She Becomes Organic Farmer, Merchant, Too." *Christian Science Monitor,* 20 November 1979.

Through a program run by the Pike Place Market Preservation and Development Authority in Seattle, Washington, to get people back to the land, Donna Osseward recently converted herself from a computer programmer to a farmer.

571 Silber, Terry. *A Small Farm in Maine.* Boston: Houghton Mifflin Co., 1988.

The author was the art director for the *Atlantic* before becoming a full-time farmer in Maine. This book details her early adaptations to rural life and later integration of urban skills into her new agricultural milieu.

572 Staudt, Kathleen A. "Class and Sex in the Politics of Women Farmers." *Journal of Politics* 41, no. 2 (1979): 492-512.

573 Tallman, Viviane Peter. "Farmer Tallman and Her Girls." *Ms.,* April 1986, pp. 55-57.

A brief portrait of a woman who took up dairy farming in Oregon and who discovered both hardships and rewards.

574 Taylor, Georgina M. "Gladys Strum: Farm Woman, Teacher, and Politician." *Canadian Women's Studies* 7, no. 4 (Winter 1986): 89-93.

575 Vold, Mona. "This Land Is Their Land." *Ms.,* November 1987, pp. 76-82.

This is about farm women and women farmers who "deal with disillusionment, argue past-due notices at the bank, take on the traditionally male-only responsibilities of the farm, organize protest sales, and lobby for legislation at state capitals," in order to keep their family farms.

Resources on Intersecting Issues of Concern

The life of women in the corporation was influenced by the proportions in which they found themselves. Those women who were few in number among male peers and often had "only woman" status became tokens: symbols of how-women-can-do, stand-ins for all women. Sometimes they had the advantages of those who are "different" and thus were highly visible in a system where success is tied to becoming known. Sometimes they faced the loneliness of the outsider, of the stranger who intrudes upon an alien culture and may become self-estranged in the process of assimilation. In any case, their turnover and "failure rate" were known to be much higher than those of men in entry and early-grade positions; in the sales function, women's turnover was twice that of men. What happened around Indsco [Industrial Supply Corporation] women resembled other reports of experiences of women in politics, law, medicine or management who have been the few among many men.

> –Rosabeth Moss Kanter,
> *Men and Women of the*
> *Corporation*, 1977

Any study of women at work is fundamentally interdisciplinary, and this bibliographical study has been especially so. One does not inquire about a woman in a nontraditional field without immediately encountering powerful sociological, psychological, philosophical, economic, and historical issues of significance. This section highlights the intersecting issues of workplace social and structural change, occupational and sex segregation, career and vocational education, books for children about women at work in nontraditional fields, the experiences of women of color in their nontraditional work, and general further reading about women and work.

Changing Institutions

In spite of the persistent nature of discrimination, significant effort is being made by selected employers to address women's workplace needs in nontraditional settings. The following references are included in the hope that more employers will try new strategies to address positive change, based on new understanding both of research findings and of the reported field experience.

576 Arvey, Richard D. "Sex Bias in Job Evaluation Procedures." *Personnel Psychology* 39 (1986): 315-35.

Arvey surveys the literature on sex bias in job evaluation procedures and gives insight into the actual points in an evaluation where bias is apt to arise. He is not considering performance evaluation in this article; he is looking at the techniques evaluators use to determine the work of a job. He considers the different approaches to evaluation of female-dominated jobs and male-dominated ones and identifies many points where bias can definitely influence an evaluator's findings.

577 Bem, S.L. "Beyond Androgyny: Some Presumptuous Prescriptions for a Liberated Sexual Identity." In *The Psychology of Women: Future Directions in Research,* edited by Julia A. Sherman and Florence L. Denmark. New York: Psychological Dimensions, 1978.

Set against the debilitating effects of sex-role stereotyping, Bem wants to free the human personality from the restricting prison of sex-role stereotyping and to develop a conception of mental health that is free from culturally imposed definitions of masculinity and femininity. She discusses the appropriate blending of masculine and feminine traits in all people.

578 Brannon, Robert. "Measuring Attitudes toward Women (and Otherwise): A Methodological Critique." In *The Psychology of Women: Future Directions in Research,* edited by Julia A. Sherman and Florence L. Denmark. New York: Psychological Dimensions, 1978.

This is a lengthy introduction to the author's view that conceptual and methodological errors are being made in the developing area of measuring attitudes and other dispositions toward and about women.

579 Carroll, S.J. "Women Candidates and Support for Feminist Concerns: The Closet Feminist Syndrome." *Western Political Quarterly* 37 (June 1984): 307-323.

Carroll discusses women in political leadership positions who identify with women's issues but who do not feel safe admitting their support publicly. She names this phenomenon the "closet feminist syndrome" and suggests its implications. (Author's note: This syndrome exists in many of the nontraditional fields for women, but it has not been so named.)

580 Fairhurst, Gail Theus, and Snavely, B. Kay. "Majority and Token Minority Group Relationships: Power Acquisition and Communication." *Academy of Management Review* 8, no. 2 (April 1983): 292-300.

The authors raise several counterattacks on Kanter's theory of tokenism. They suggest that individual responses to the token role can vary with a consideration of power and status. Their suggestion is that tokens have more power than they or their organizations think they do. This is a theoretical discussion that does not test its hypotheses in an empirical setting.

581 Fennell, M.L., Barchas, P.R., et al. "An Alternative Perspective on Sex Differences in Organizational Settings: The Process of Legitimation." *Sex Roles,* no. 4 (1978): 589-603.

This article presents a new perspective on working relationships between men and women in the workplace. The authors reject sex-role socialization as a reason for different behavior and instead explore the structural arrangements of organizations. Intervention strategies, which employers may wish to consider if they are serious about equalizing relationships between women and men in the workplace, are outlined at the end of the article.

582 Good, J., Kirkland, F.R., et al. *Working Relationships between Men and Women: Effects of Sex and Hierarchical Position on Perceptions of Self and Others in a Work Setting.* Technical Report no. 6. Philadelphia: University City Science Center, 1979.

Cooper (see entry 7) reports that "experience in mixed-sex groups results in higher ratings of each sex by the other."

583　Harrison, Evelyn. "Working Women: Barriers in Employment."
　　　　Public Administration Review 24 (June 1964): 78-85.

　　　　　　Harrison begins her article with the statement that what
　　　women want and need is not as dramatic as what the American Negro
　　　wants and needs today. She states that Negroes are struggling for full
　　　rights as citizens and in contrast what women want is freedom from
　　　social, economic, and legal restrictions imposed by prejudice or
　　　outmoded custom. Women want to overcome the discriminations
　　　imposed on them, she says, by "lingering memories of an antiquated
　　　social pattern and adherence to romantic but unrealistic stereotypes of
　　　what woman's role should be in modern life." Thus Harrison begins a
　　　lucid explanation of barriers to women in the work force and some
　　　governmental initiatives to modify them. The article gives interesting
　　　insight into the psychology of the day in which the barriers were
　　　identified and simultaneously downplayed as not as serious as needing
　　　full rights as citizens.

584　Hoffman, Lois Wladis. "Effects of Maternal Employment on the
　　　　Child: A Review of the Research." *Developmental Psychology* 10
　　　　(1974): 204-28.

　　　　　　Hoffman explores the vast literature of maternal employment
　　　and its effect on children and organizes her findings around five
　　　hypotheses: 1. The working mother provides a different role model than
　　　the nonworking mother does. 2. Employment affects the mother's
　　　emotional state, sometimes providing satisfactions, sometimes role
　　　strain, sometimes guilt. 3. The different situational demands as well as
　　　the emotional state of the working mother affect child-rearing
　　　practices. 4. Working mothers provide less adequate supervision. 5. The
　　　working mother's absence results in emotional and possibly cognitive
　　　deprivation for the child. The findings regarding the working mother as
　　　role model are significant to this inquiry about women in nontraditional
　　　fields. Particularly interesting was a mention of a study by J.K. Baruch
　　　(*Developmental Psychology* 6 [1972]: 32-37) in which eleven college
　　　women were administered a measure developed by Goldberg in which
　　　subjects are presented with a number of journal articles and asked to
　　　judge the quality of the article and the author. Half the articles are
　　　given female names as authors and half are given male names. Previous
　　　research by Goldberg had indicated that college women tend to attach
　　　a lower value to the articles attributed to women authors. Baruch found
　　　that the daughters of employed women were significantly different from
　　　the daughters of full-time housewives, in that they did not downgrade
　　　the articles attributed to women.

585   Horner, Matina. "Fail, Bright Woman." *Psychology Today* 3, no. 6 (1969): 36-38.

Horner, former president of prestigious Radcliffe College, discusses her exploration of the reason for sex difference in achievement motivation. Her discovery of the way the achievement motive becomes contaminated by fear of success in women is now legendary, more than twenty years later.

586   Kanter, Rosabeth Moss. "Some Effects of Proportions on Group Life: Skewed Sex Ratios and Responses to Token Women." *American Journal of Sociology* 82 (1977): 965-90.

A framework for conceptualizing the processes that occur between dominants and tokens in organizations is established in this article. The paper addresses itself to issues of proportion in social life and clarifies their significance. Four groups are set forth in the article: uniform groups, skewed groups, titled groups, and balanced groups.

587   Kerr, Barbara A. *Smart Girls, Gifted Women.* Columbus: Ohio Psychology Publishing Co., 1985.

An important book, in part because Kerr outlines the barriers to achievement gifted women encounter in their development. Her analysis of the external barriers finds parallels in the lives of average women, and her analysis of internal barriers is likewise applicable to other women. One wonders how many women who enter nontraditional fields are gifted.

588   Laws, Judith Long. "The Psychology of Tokenism: An Analysis." *Sex Roles* 1, no. 1 (1975): 51-67.

This article is heavily quoted in the literature and is seminal in its insights. Laws discusses tokenism in the academic profession. She traces a developmental history of a woman who becomes a token in academic life, and clarifies the acquisition of attitudes along the way. Laws identifies an early sponsor, usually female, when the woman is growing up. Then, she identifies a second sponsor, invariably male, who adopts this role in a departmental setting where she studies. Laws clarifies the specifications of the role bargain including exceptionalism and individualism, and she also discusses boundary maintenance. Overall, she finds that the role of token is impossible without the corresponding role of sponsor.

589   Lever, Janet, and Schwartz, Pepper. *Women at Yale: Liberating a College Campus.* Indianapolis: Bobbs-Merrill Co., 1971.

In the late 1960s two young women from a coeducational university in the Midwest became graduate students in sociology at Yale as the campus was converting to coeducation. They decided this environment, previously all-male, needed scientific study. They analyzed the "male mystique of Yale" to find out the characteristics of its environment that were similar to other all-male institutions, and how the campus would adjust to the addition of women. In this book, Janet Lever and Pepper Schwartz study and analyze one year at Yale and draw some fascinating conclusions about the social dynamics of sexual integration. Recommended for everyone interested in a "super male atmosphere" that is changed forever by the presence of smart women.

590   Miles, Mary. "Do You Treat Women Employees Different from the Men?" *Computer Decisions* 16, no. 5 (April 1984): 80-88.

This article contains an open discussion of the ways managers are revising traditional ways of treating female employees in corporate settings. Reference is made to some men who "may be straddling the gender gap rather awkwardly." Human resources management techniques are spelled out, including: applying equal standards to both women and men; never making assumptions about women, such as that they are not mobile, are too emotional, or lack career commitment; improving the quality of recruitment at the entry level and involving senior managers in the key task of campus recruitment; improving the quality of the image of the company and the field itself; and recognizing the importance of a professional human resources department that identifies and develops high-potential individuals, regardless of sex.

591   Piliavin, Jane Allyn, and Martin, Rachel Rosemann. "The Effects of Sex Composition of Groups on Style of Social Interaction." *Sex Roles,* no. 4 (1978): 281-96.

In this study, eighty-four-person discussion groups were run: sixteen all-female, sixteen all-male, and forty-eight mixed-sex (two males and two females). The authors say "the strongest and clearest finding is that the behavior of individuals in groups is determined to a much greater degree by their sex than by the composition of the group in which they are interacting. In general females interacting in groups with males perform in a somewhat more task-oriented and less socioemotional way than they do in all-female groups."

592   Plas, Jeanne M., and Wallston, Barbara Strudler. "Women Oriented
toward Male-Dominated Careers: Is the Reference Group Male or
Female?" *Journal of Counseling Psychology* 30, no. 1 (1983): 46-54.

This study collected data about the networks of women
interested in role-innovative careers and asked the following questions.
Are the levels of self-valuing of these women related more significantly
to the amount of support they receive from men and women? Is their
self-esteem associated more primarily with their levels of regard for
women or men? Are their patterns of encouraging males and females
of differential importance to their levels of self-esteem?

Plas and her colleagues found that the women in the study who
showed higher levels of self-esteem reported greater value and
encouragement of women and thought women were important to their
interpersonal worlds. They note that women who seek success in male-
dominated fields and who wish to avoid the role of token may benefit
from knowing that positive attitudes toward other women may increase
their own self-value.

593   Pleck, Joseph H. "Males' Traditional Attitudes toward Women:
Conceptual Issues in Research." In *The Psychology of Women:
Future Directions in Research,* edited by Julia A. Sherman and
Florence L. Denmark. New York: Psychological Dimensions, 1978.

Pleck's analysis concludes that "there is no sharp demarcation
of male vs. female attitudes toward women on any clear dimension."

594   Smith, E.R., Ferree, M.M., and Miller, F.D. "Short Scale of
Attitudes toward Feminism." *Representative Research in Social
Psychology,* no. 6 (1975): 51-56.

In 1975, the authors concluded that the growing interest in the
psychology of women and sex roles required tools for research studies.
So they updated a scale of attitudes toward feminism that was
developed in 1936 by C. Kirkpatrick. They tested their scale thoroughly
with undergraduate psychology students at an Ivy League college and
with students in summer school at Harvard (ages 15-34) and with an
almost equal balance between men and women. They stress that this is
a test of attitudes toward feminism, not toward avowed feminists. They
wanted to be able to assess acceptance of feminist beliefs. They say,
"This distinction is important as one would expect attitudes toward
feminism to predict many behaviors, such as cooperativeness toward
women, or support for equal-rights legislation." One wonders what the

findings would be if this scale were administered to a cross section of representative women in all kinds of nontraditional fields.

595 Wolman, C., and Frank, H. "The Solo Woman in a Professional Peer Group." *American Journal of Orthopsychiatry*, no. 45 (1975): 164-71.

    The paper analyzes six peer groups of graduate students of psychiatric residents, each containing one woman. Wolman and Frank trace the group's behavior patterns in reaction to the inclusion of a female member. The results are disastrous for each woman as no matter what she does she is trivialized through the group process. The authors propose one outrageous alternative for solo women: "Decrease all behavior for a long time." Although the paper gives insights into men's group behavior, overall it is very discouraging about the possibility of improvement in the social dynamics for women, unless their numbers in the group are increased significantly.

596 Yoder, Janice D., and Prince, H.T. "The Price of a Token." *Journal of Political and Military Sociology* 11 (1983): 325-37.

    This paper examines West Point, where more-experienced women cadets failed to sponsor incoming freshwomen. Paper tries to uncover the situational contingencies that make the role of the successful token woman inhibitive to the sponsorship of future generations of female professionals. The contingencies include: performance pressures of tokenism; persistently marginal status of tokens; doubts about peer acceptance; tokens' reluctance to forfeit the specialness of visibility; uncertainties about the new and different freshwomen; and the role encapsulation of token women into stereotypically feminine positions that preclude mentoring. Article contains extensive and detailed discussion of the situational constraints, and it argues for structural and organizational changes, rather than changes directed at altering or accommodating individuals to an existent system, as the first step in admitting hitherto-excluded groups to an exclusive organization.

597 Yoder, Janice D., et al. "To Teach Is to Learn: Overcoming Tokenism with Mentors." *Psychology of Women Quarterly* 9 (March 1985): 119-31.

    About the lack of mentors in nontraditional job areas and the need for development of them.

Women of Color at Work in Nontraditional Fields

These materials are supplemented by others found throughout the book.

598   Almquist, Elizabeth, and Wehrle-Einhorn, Juanita. "The Doubly Disadvantaged: Minority Women in the Labor Force." In *Women Working,* edited by Ann H. Stromberg and Shirley Harkness. Palo Alto, Calif.: Mayfield, 1978.
      A good overview of issues, particularly for Hispanic women.

599   Burlew, Ann Kathleen. "The Experiences of Black Females in Traditional and Nontraditional Professions." *Psychology of Women Quarterly* 6, no. 3 (Spring 1982): 312-26.
      Burlew found that there are important differences between black women pursuing traditional and nontraditional careers. She found that black women with early work experience were more likely to select nontraditional careers than black women who had not worked before. (For further annotation, see entry 263).

600   *Conference on Educational and Occupational Needs of Asian-Pacific American Women, 24-25 August 1976.* Washington, D.C.: National Institute of Education, 1980.
      Conference proceedings.

601   Davis, M.S. "Sex-Role Factors in the Career Development of Black Female High School Students." Ph.D. dissertation, University of Cincinnati, 1977.

602   Enstad, Robert. "In Smashing Atoms, Woman Breaks a Barrier." *Chicago Tribune,* 14 June 1985.
      Teresa Duncan, a black woman now graduating from Northwestern University, is believed to be the first black woman in the nation with a degree in nuclear engineering.

603   Epstein, Cynthia Fuchs. "Black and Female: the Double Whammy." *Psychology Today,* August 1973, pp. 57-89.

Burlew cites Epstein as a researcher who noted that those few women who have careers in nontraditional areas "impress others with their self-confidence." The author discusses the strengths she sees in black women professionals, including an ability to combine home and work life and a relative absence of self-doubt.

604   Gump, Janice Porter. "Reality and Myth: Employment and Sex-Role Ideology in Black Women." In *The Psychology of Women: Future Directions in Research,* edited by Julia A. Sherman and Florence L. Denmark. New York: Psychological Dimensions, 1978.

The author, a black clinical psychologist, begins this article thus: "The traditional role does not exist for the black woman." She discusses sex-role expectations, strains, and satisfactions for black women in the work world. She gives critical insights into the different norms for black and white women, career patterns for black and white women, comparative economic needs, labor-force participation rates, occupational choices, and approaches to working and motherhood, and she provides an excellent two-page list of references that are instructive for a person interested in further information about the black woman in the work force.

605   Gurin, P., and Epps, E. *Black Consciousness, Identity, and Achievement.* New York: Wiley & Sons, 1975.

Insight into how black women choose their careers. Suggests that the same sex-role constraints operating as boundaries for white women influence black women.

606   Hess-Biber, Sharlene. "The Black Woman Worker: A Minority Group Perspective on Women at Work." *Sage: A Scholarly Journal on Black Women* 3, no. 1 (Spring 1986): 26-34.

607   Kim, Elaine H., and Otani, Janice. *With Silk Wings: Asian-American Women at Work.* El Cerrito, Calif.: Asian Women United of California, 1983.

Fifty-two profiles of women in many fields; brief historical essay at end on Asian women in the United States. There are also two films by the same title made in 1982 by this same group. All of these works document Asian-American women's experiences of work in nontraditional fields.

608 Mednick, M., and Puryear, G. "Motivational and Personality Factors Related to Career Goals of Black College Women." *Journal of Social and Behavioral Science* 21 (1975): 1-30.

Found that expectations of black women pursuing traditional careers and those pursuing nontraditional careers were different. Those pursuing nontraditional careers were expecting self-oriented satisfactions; they perceived their choices as ideal but they were not blind to the obstacles ahead. According to Burlew, Mednick and Puryear did not find evidence that black female innovators worry about the incompatibility of their careers with marriage. Rather, black female innovators, according to Burlew's reading, planned a lifetime of work . . . and did not express much worry about combining work and marriage.

609 National Committee on Pay Equity. *Pay Equity: An Issue of Race, Ethnicity, and Sex.* Washington, D.C.: National Committee on Pay Equity, 1987.

The committee (located at 1201 16th Street NW, Washington, D.C.) is comprised of representatives from many civil rights and women's organizations. It is a 501c3 tax-exempt corporation. Contributors include representatives from the Center for Research on Women at Memphis State University, Center for Women in Government at the Institute for Government and Policy Studies at Rockefeller College, State University for New York at Albany, the Equal Employment and Affirmative Action Office and the Women's Information Center of the University of Washington, and the Service Employees International Union. The book includes studies on pay equity as a remedy for race and sex discrimination. Each study is based in different regions of the country.

610 Newman, Debra Lynn. "Black Women Workers in the Twentieth Century." *Sage: A Scholarly Journal on Black Women* 3, no. 1 (Spring 1986): 10-15.

611   Wallace, Phyllis A. *Black Women in the Labor Force.* Cambridge, Mass.: MIT Press, 1980.

A fascinating and important book about black working women.

612   Weathers, Diane. "The Working Woman and the Men in Her Life." *Black Enterprise,* August 1977, pp. 14-17, 50.

A brief analysis of the many differences between black and white women in the work force. The article makes reference to the work of researchers interested in black working women: black sociologist Joyce Ladner Carrington; economist Barbara Jones; psychologist Jacqueline Fleming; and Marion Kilson, who was director of research for the Radcliffe Institute in Cambridge, Mass., at the time that the article was written. The article also explores personal relationships between black women and black men and identifies this as a critical issue.

Sex Segregation/Occupational Segregation

613   Acker, Joan, and Van Houten, Donald. "The Sex Structure of Organizations: Selective Recruitment and Control." *Administrative Science Quarterly* 19 (June 1974): 152-62.

An analysis of tracking systems for men and women in organizational life.

614   Bass, Bernard, Krusell, Judith, and Alexander, Ralph. "Male Managers' Attitudes toward Working Women." *American Behavioral Scientist* 15 (November-December 1971): 221-36.

615   Bielby, William T., and Baron, James A. "Men and Women at Work: Sex Segregation and Statistical Discrimination." *American Journal of Sociology* 91, no. 4 (January 1986): 759-99.

This article describes research that tests hypotheses about reasons for sex segregation in occupations employing both men and women. They find that "work done by both men and women is often done in distinct organizational settings, and when enterprises employ both sexes in the same occupation, they typically assign them different job titles." The authors recommend several research initiatives based on their findings: analyses of the role played by employers' beliefs and perceptions are needed and studies of the institutionalization of gender-based employment practices are also advisable.

616   Blau, Francine D. "The Data on Women Workers Past, Present, and Future." In *Women Working*, edited by Ann H. Stromberg and Shirley Harkness. Palo Alto, Calif.: Mayfield, 1978.

617   Blau, Francine D., and Ferber, Marianne A. "Women in the Labor Market: The Last Twenty Years." In *Women and Work: An Annual Review*, vol. 1, edited by Laurie Larwood, Ann H. Stromberg, and Barbara A. Gutek. Beverly Hills, Calif.: Sage, 1985.
      This article examines the last twenty years in regard to labor-force participation of women, labor-force attachment, the allocation of time of men and women between the household and the labor market, occupational segregation, and the earnings gap.

618   Blaxall, Martha, and Reagan, Barbara, eds. *Women and the Workplace: The Implications of Occupational Segregation*. Chicago: University of Chicago Press, 1976.
      The implications of occupational segregation are discussed in sixteen essays by various social scientists, including Jean Lipmen-Blumen, Judith Long Laws, Margaret J. Gates, Heidi Hartmann, and Francine Blau. Responses to many of the essays are included.
      The papers and comments in this book are expanded from the proceedings of a conference on occupational segregation held in May 1975. It was jointly sponsored by the American Economic Association and the Center for Research on Women in Higher Education and the Professions at Wellsley College. The book is highly recommended to all readers.

619   Chertos, Cynthia, Haignere, Lois, and Steinberg, Ronnie. eds. *Occupational Segregation and Its Impact on Working Women: A Conference Report*. Report of a conference held at the Ford Foundation, 9 June 1982. Albany: State University of New York, Center for Women in Government, 1982.
      Discusses nontraditional occupations, among other subjects.

620   Ferber, Marianne A. "Women and Work: Issues of the 1980s." *Signs* 8, no. 2 (Winter 1982): 273-95.

   A review and analysis of pertinent research findings in the economics literature. Her discussion of economists' consideration of issues of sexual and occupational segregation and discrimination is particularly relevant to this study. (See entry 702 for further annotation.)

621   Fox, Mary Frank, and Hess-Biber, Sharlene. *Women at Work.* Palo Alto, Calif.: Mayfield, 1984.

   An excellent feminist analysis of basic issues regarding women at work. Contains a perceptive chapter on minority women.

622   Goffman, Erving. *Stigma: Notes on the Management of a Spoiled Identity.* Englewood Cliffs, N.J.: Prentice-Hall, 1963.

623   Goldman, Paul. "The Organizational Caste System and the New Working Class." *Insurgent Sociologist* 3 (Winter 1973): 41-51.

624   Gross, Edward. "Plus ça change . . . ? The Sexual Structure of Occupations over Time." *Social Problems* 16 (Fall 1968): 198-208.

625   Hartmann, Heidi. "Capitalism, Patriarchy, and Job Segregation by Sex." *Signs: A Journal of Women in Culture and Society* 1 (Spring 1976): 137-69.

   Hartmann explains the historical roots of occupational segregation. An important feminist analysis.

626   Haven, E.W. "Factors Associated with the Selection of Advanced Mathematics Courses by Girls in High School." Ph.D. dissertation, University of Pennsylvania, 1971.

627 Kanter, Rosabeth Moss. "Women and the Structure of Organizations." In *Another Voice: Feminist Perspectives on Social Life and Social Science,* edited by Jon R. Kanter and M. Millman. New York: Doubleday, 1975.
    An important analysis.

628 Kessler-Harris, Alice. "The Debate over Equality for Women in the Workplace: Recognized Differences." In *Women and Work: An Annual Review,* vol. 1, edited by Laurie Larwood, Ann H. Stromberg, and Barbara A. Gutek. Beverly Hills, Calif.: Sage, 1985.
    Kessler-Harris discusses whether women are really different from men in the workplace. She suggests that recognizing and accepting differences may lead more rapidly to true equality. Kessler-Harris traces the history of working women in the late nineteenth century and early twentieth. She describes a conflict among women themselves. Some favored full equality where human rights transcended any biological difference. Others insisted that women were different and that they required special protection. She then traces the history of these two ideas as the twentieth century progressed and points out that the conflict has still not been resolved. Kessler-Harris interprets a modern version of "difference acceptance" by suggesting that what had once been considered private issues regarding family and home are now issues in the public workplace. She thinks this view holds the potential for achieving true equality. She says: "It opens up the possibility that an ethic of compassion or tolerance, a sense of group responsibility to the world at large (instead of to self) might in fact penetrate the workplace."

629 Kessler-Harris, Alice. "Stratifying by Sex: Understanding the History of Working Women." In *Labor Market Segmentation,* edited by R. Edwards, M. Reich, and D. Gordon. Lexington, Mass.: D.C. Heath, 1975.

630 Lipmen-Blumen, Jean. "Toward a Homosocial Theory of Sex Roles: An Explanation of the Sex Segregation of Social Institutions." *Signs* 1 (Spring 1976): 15-31.
    A discussion of single-sex socializing among men suggesting its influence on the perpetuation of sex segregation at work.

631   Mechanic, David. "Sources of Power to Lower-Level Participants." *Administrative Science Quarterly* 7 (December 1962): 349-64.

632   Miller, Jon, and Labovitz, Sanford. "Inequities in Organizations: Experiences of Men and Women." *Social Forces* 54 (December 1975): 365-79.
      An analysis of the way women are treated differently than men in bureaucratic organizations.

633   Oppenheimer, Valerie. *The Female Labor Force in the United States.* Berkeley: University of California Press, 1970.
      About structure based on gender in work environment.

634   Pogrebin, Letty Cottin. "The Intimate Politics of Working with Men." *Ms.,* October 1975, pp. 48-51, 96, 105-106.
      A discussion of the perceived dangers, particularly of sexual intimacy, when men and women work together.

635   Reskin, Barbara F., ed. *Sex Segregation in the Workplace: Trends, Explanations, Remedies.* Washington, D.C.: National Academy Press, 1984.
      Has a section called "Reducing Segregation: The Effectiveness of Integration."

636   Reskin, Barbara F., and Hartmann, Heidi, eds. *Women's Work, Men's Work: Sex Segregation on the Job.* Washington, D.C.: National Academy Press, 1986.
      A useful analysis. See entry 725 for full annotation.

637   U.S. Department of Labor. "Update on Employment Structure and Earning Trends." Washington, D.C.: U.S. Government Printing Office, 1979.
      Mentioned in newsletter called *Choices,* Midwest Sex Desegregation Assistance Center, 1627 Anderson Avenue, Manhattan, KS 66505.

638 Wolf, Wendy C., and Fligstein, Neil D. "Sex and Authority in the Workplace: The Causes of Sexual Inequality." *American Sociological Review* 44 (1979): 235-52.

639 Wolf, Wendy C., and Rosenfeld, Rachel Ann. "Sex Structure of Occupations and Job Mobility." *Social Forces* 56 (1978): 823-44.

Career Counseling/Vocational Education

The interactions that take place between counselors in vocational and career centers and women in search of working options are often highly influential in women's lives. If the advice given is based on limited awareness of the growing opportunities for women in hundreds of different fields, or worse, is based on biased or out-of-date views of what is appropriate work for women, much talent is tragically wasted while sex stereotypes of occupations prevail.

This list of materials is included as a partial guide to the literature of the changing nature of job choice and to gender-neutral sources of information.

640 Beyea, Patricia, and O'Kane, Geraldine. *How to Erase Sex Discrimination in Vocational Education.* New York: American Civil Liberties Union (ACLU) Foundation, Women's Rights Project, September 1977, 77 pp.

Excellent photos on cover. One, a girl of about six or seven is sawing through a piece of wood. The other is a girl of about the same age hammering long nails into a piece of wood. Contents include: why vocational education is a big (and sex-discriminatory) business; the structure of the vocational-education establishment; how to gather facts about vocational education in your area; laws against sex discrimination in vocational education; organizing a campaign against sex discrimination in vocational education; getting good media coverage; and using public education in your vocational education program. This booklet is available from the ACLU Foundation, Women's Rights Project, 22 East 40th Street, New York, NY 10016.

641 Brandt, S. J. "Psychological Correlates of Occupational Choices in Women." Ph.D. dissertation, Adelphi University, 1977.

Research shows that women with an internal locus of control were more likely to aspire to innovative occupations than were their more externally directed counterparts.

642   Burack, Elmer H., et al. *Growing: A Woman's Guide to Career Satisfaction.* Belmont, Calif.: Lifetime Learning Publications, 1980.

643   Burlin, F. D. "Locus of Control and Female Occupational Aspirations." *Journal of Counseling Psychology* 23 (1976): 123-29.

644   Burton, G. M. "The Power of the Raised Eyebrow." *School Counselor* 25, no. 2 (November 1977): 116-22.
About equal education, particularly in mathematics, for girls, and the school counselor's critical role in affirming its importance.

645   Catalyst, Inc. *Creating Change for College Women: The Catalyst Model Staff Training Program.* New York: The Catalyst Company, 1978, 94 pp.
This booklet is the culmination of two years of work to stimulate educators to create campus change regarding the career choices of undergraduates.

646   Catalyst, Inc. *It's Your Future! Catalyst's Career Guide for High School Girls.* New York: Peterson's Guides, 1984.

647   Catalyst, Inc. *What to Do with the Rest of Your Life.* New York: Simon and Schuster, 1980.

648   Costick, Rita M., et al. *Nonsexist Career Counseling for Women: Annotated Selected References and Resources, Parts I and II.* Washington, D.C.: U.S. Office of Education, 1978.

This two-part bibliography, available in ERIC (ED 158212 and ED 158213) and also distributed by the Far West Laboratory for Educational Research and Development in San Francisco, is designed to provide resources for counselors, counselor educators, teachers and others trying to facilitate positive, nonstereotyped career awareness and development of women at secondary and postsecondary levels.

649   *Directory of Career Resources for Women.* Santa Monica, Calif.: Ready Reference Press, 1979.

650   Doss, Martha Merrill, ed. *The Directory of Special Opportunities for Women.* Garrett Park, Md.: Garrett Park Press, 1981.

651   Farmer, Helen S. *New Career Options for Women: A Counselor's Sourcebook.* New York: Human Sciences Press, 1977.
       Educational materials for counselors. Now dated, but a rich compendium of timely information in the 1970s for career counselors. Individual career choices are not detailed; this is more an introduction to where to get other sources of information. Goes a long way to provide information that will help eliminate sex bias in counseling, if used.

652   Gilbert, Linda A., and Waldroop, James. "Evaluation of a Procedure for Increasing Sex-Fair Counseling." *Journal of Counseling Psychology* 25 (September 1978): 410-18.
       The authors explain a gender-neutral counseling procedure.

653   Haber, S. "Cognitive Support for the Career Choices of College Women." *Sex Roles* 6 (1980): 129-38.
       Fifty college women of lower- and middle-class backgrounds in New York City were surveyed regarding career aspirations. This researcher found that maternal employment was not as significant a determinant for this group as the parental attitudes toward role innovation and career choice. The innovative career-oriented women often had their mothers as cognitive models, a finding which suggested

that opportunities would be greater for their daughters than they were for them regardless of employment status.

654   Houser, Betsy Bosak, and Garvey, Chris. "Factors That Affect Nontraditional Vocational Enrollment among Women." *Psychology of Women Quarterly* 9 (March 1985): 105-117.
      This study examines the relationship between a young woman's career choice and several internal and external factors that are likely to affect her choice. Women who made nontraditional choices are compared with ones who made more traditional choices. The study analyzes factors such as: external-support influence; attitudes of other people close to them such as parents, teachers, and friends; sex-role orientation; locus of control; and fear of success. The study is based on a sample of 470 women who were an average of 20 years old, 73 percent white, 4 percent black, 12 percent Hispanic, 270 Asian, and 10 percent "other." Houser and Garvey found that the one dimension that differentiated the nontraditionals from the other students was the amount of support and encouragement they received from significant others in their lives. Houser and Garvey recommend in their conclusions that in order to improve educational quality and equality of opportunity, "the attention of policy makers and educational staff members should be focused on educating the family members, friends, teachers, counselors of the girls who are making career decisions." They say, "These individuals should be made aware that the majority of today's women will hold jobs outside the home and that many of these women will be the sole support of their families." Houser and Garvey also include a useful literature review in their article.

655   Kane, Roslyn D., et al. *A Model to Retrain Women Teachers and Skilled Women as Teachers in Non-Traditional Vocational Programs.* Arlington, Va.: Rj Associates, June 1977, 111 pp.
      Prepared for U.S. Department of Health, Education, and Welfare, Office of Education, Bureau of Occupational and Adult Education, Vocational Education Branch.

656   Klemmack, D. L., and Edwards, J. N. "Women's Acquisition of Stereotyped Occupational Aspirations." *Sociology and Social Research* 57 (1973): 1973.
      Published in the early 1970s, this article discusses the emerging role expansions of women as changes from "feminine" to "modern" sex

roles. The authors discuss the nature of women's occupational aspirations and the type of occupations they will pursue. Data were secured from 300 women at a land-grant university. Terminology such as "degree of femininity in occupational aspiration" was not clearly defined in the article, nor was the phrase "least-feminine occupations." One interesting finding of the study was that approximately half of those studied indicated a preference for a nontraditional field.

657 Lee, Chris. "Training for Women: Where Do We Go from Here?" *Training,* December 1986, pp. 26-40.

An extensive, thoughtful article about the subtle, institutionalized barriers women face in the business world as they try to achieve full equality. The article is also about training women to deal with these elusive forms of discrimination. There is a center feature in this article entitled, "Historical Perspective on the Woman Question." It outlines the public-policy debates on many related questions.

658 Medema, Marcia, et al. *First Step: A Manual for Career Development and Job-Seeking Skills.* Chicago: Midwest Women's Center, 1986.

Seven chapters in a ring binder proceeding from defining your desires to reviewing your decisions.

659 National Council on the Future of Women in the Workplace. *Taking Action on Career Counseling: A Guide for Volunteers.* Introduction by Eleanor Holmes Norton. Washington, D.C.: Business and Professional Women's Foundation, 1985.

An excellent manual for community volunteers to use as they tackle the challenge of career counseling for girls.

660 The National Council on the Future of Women in the Workplace and Girls Clubs of America, Inc. *Women Helping Girls with Choices.* Washington, D.C.: Elaine Reuben Associates, April 1986, 30 pp.

This is a manual for community women to use in projects of various kinds that prepare girls for their long future in the workplace. It explains one pilot project in New Hampshire, and it suggests ways to take action in the community. It has an excellent resource chapter containing information on print and film materials to support community education. The booklet also clarifies some special needs of girls, including their need to value themselves, their need for nurturance and nonjudgmental relationships, and their needs for decision-making skills, practice in meeting their own needs, and experiences in environments where they are taken seriously.

661   Osborn, Ruth Helen. *Developing New Horizons for Women.* New York: McGraw-Hill, 1977.

662   Phelps, Ann T., Farmer, Helen S., and Backer, Thomas E. *New Career Options for Women: A Selected Annotated Bibliography.* New York: Human Science Press, 1977.
This book provides a good look as of 1977 at the literature for career counselors helping women entering the world of work. Highly recommended. (For a full annotation, see entry 22.)

663   Rj Associates, Inc. *A Study of the Factors Influencing the Participation of Women in Non-Traditional Occupations in Postsecondary Vocational Training Schools.* Arlington, Va.: Rj Associates, 1976.
This report was prepared by the staff of the consulting firm Rj Associates under the direction of Roslyn D. Kane, president. A good analysis. Examined at Business and Professional Women's Foundation Library, Washington, D.C.

664   Scholz, Nelle, Prince, Judith, and Miller, Gordon. *How to Decide: A Guide for Women.* New York: College Entrance Examination Board, 1975.

665   "Sex Equity: Are Students Free to Choose?" *Vocational Education* 55 (April 1980): 17-45.

666   Slaney, Robert B., and Caballero, Mercé. "Changing Male Attitudes toward Women's Career Development: An Exploratory Study." *Journal of Counseling Psychology* 30, no. 1 (January 1983): 126-29.

In this article, Slaney and Caballero first discuss the literature of men's influence on the career development of women. They conclude that men have a very significant influence indeed, especially as partners or husbands. They then discuss whether the attitudes of men toward women's career development would be affected by the observation of videotapes from Project Born Free. They conclude that the undergraduate men studied were relatively liberal in their attitudes toward the career development of imagined wives. They concede that they cannot be sure of what their attitudes would be if they had actual wives.

667   Stahl, Patricia, ed. *New Steps on the Career Ladder.* Vol. 1, *Curriculum Guide.* Vol. 2, *Program Model and Resource Guide.* Springfield: Illinois State Board of Education, 1980.

Patricia Stahl was development and production editor for this two-volume manual. Midwest Women's Center in Chicago sponsors day-long conferences on moving into nontraditional fields, and this manual is used as part of the training material.

668   Stockton, N., Berry, J., Shepson, J., and Utz, P. "Sex Role and Innovative Major among College Students." *Journal of Vocational Behavior* 16 (1980): 360-67.

Building on the Janico study cited elsewhere in this bibliography, Stockton et al. wished to extend the study to a broader population and to more areas of academic concentration. Their sample included 693 male and female students enrolled in both traditional and unusual majors. They found that sex role seemed to have more power in the discriminant function than did sex in choice of innovative or traditional major. The authors stress that these findings are important for vocational counselors, faculty, or others who confer with students about their choices of major or career choices. The students who see themselves as more flexible in regard to sex roles have an easier time thinking more broadly about their choices.

669   Swerdloff, Sol. "Job Opportunities for Women College Graduates." *Monthly Labor Review* 87, no. 4 (April 1964): 396-400.

Interesting reading not only for the statistics of the time but also for the analysis of issues for women who choose to work after earning a college degree. Almost twenty-five years ago, the author pointed out that the statistics indicated college women should plan in college for a career, strive for high academic performance, go on to specialized graduate training where possible, and prepare to compete with men for room at the top.

670   Tangri, Sandra Schwartz. "Determinants of Occupational Role Innovation among College Women." *Journal of Social Issues* 28, no. 2 (1972): 177-99.

The author lays to rest widely accepted notions that women who enter nontraditional work are more identified with their fathers than with their mothers. She did not find that role innovators thought of themselves as masculine or made occupational plans because of difficulty in attracting the opposite sex. She did find greater characteristics of autonomy, individualism, and motivation to perform by internally imposed demands. These characteristics were coupled with doubts about ability to succeed and identity. Tolerant or supportive boyfriends were found to be important to many of the 200 college seniors in the sample.

671   Thomas, A. H., and Stewart, N. R. "Counselor Response to Female Clients with Deviate and Conforming Career Goals." *Journal of Counseling Psychology* 18 (1971): 352-57.

The authors studied whether secondary school counselors respond more positively to female clients with traditionally feminine (i.e., conforming) goals than those with traditionally masculine (or deviate) goals. They found that counselors, regardless of sex, rated conforming goals as more appropriate for women and that counselors of both sexes felt women with deviate career goals were more in need of counseling than those with conforming goals. While the authors suggest that counselors are only human and in conflict about whether to act as agents of change or agents of conformity, the effects on the women themselves are not considered. One wonders how many women have been discouraged from further consideration of a nontraditional goal by a counselor who felt it was deviate and therefore not advisable.

672   University of North Carolina, Chapel Hill. School of Education. "Becoming: A Leader's Guide for High School Graduates." Newton, Mass.: Women's Educational Equity Act Publishing Center, 1980.

Workshop materials, compiled by Dr. Nancy L. Voight, to help participants examine personality, values, how to deal with discrimination, decision making, and job search skills.

673 Warren, James. "City Trade School Threatened on Sex Bias." *Chicago Tribune,* 1 April 1986.

In 1984, five women filed a complaint with the federal government alleging sex discrimination in all aspects of the programs at the Washburne Trade School in Chicago. The U.S. Office of Education and the Office of Civil Rights found widespread evidence of sex discrimination against female students in admissions, counseling, and placement at the school. Government officials concluded that the school had "engendered an atmosphere of sexual isolation and harassment." At the time of this article, Washburne officials were said to be acting with a sense of purpose and urgency to correct the deficits found in their programs.

674 Women's Work Force. *National Directory of Women's Employment Programs: Who They Are; What They Do.* Washington, D.C.: Wider Opportunities for Women, 1979.

Part 1 features techniques for counselor training/professional development, including research, models, strategies, and techniques in career counseling for women; resources for nonsexist career counseling; ways to measure women's career interest; information on career counseling and minority women. Part 2 includes sections on women and work, women in specific occupations and professions, and programs related to women's career preparation and training.

Children's Books

One year the rabbinic team consisted of three women. As the three of us conducted high holiday services, I snapped a mental picture: There we were, draped in our ritual prayer shawls, one of us holding the Torah, one of us chanting the haunting high holiday melodies, and one holding the ram's horn. In front of us were the 30 children of the congregation, beaming, expectant. And I knew they were not thinking 'lady rabbis.' To them, this is Judaism. The children are growing up with the changes we have struggled to create.

–Rabbi Julie Greenberg,
Washington Post, 1989

In the spirit of raising children free of sex-role expectations regarding work choice, the following books introduce readers to women doing their chosen work without suggesting that it is in any way unusual.

675   Ashby, Marylee S., and Wittmaier, Bruce C. "Attitude Changes in Children after Exposure to Stories about Women in Traditional or Nontraditional Occupations." *Journal of Educational Psychology* 70 (December 1978): 945-49.

Ashby and Wittmaier conclude that "one cannot expose girls to sexist books throughout childhood and then grant them a 'free' choice of the role they want as an adult because such choices will not actually be free." In this research, they clarify the importance of nonsexist books and textbooks in widening girls' aspirations and self-images.

676   Bracken, Jeanne, and Wigutoff, Sharon. *Books for Today's Young Readers: An Annotated Bibliography of Recommended Fiction for Ages 10-14.* Old Westbury, N.Y.: Feminist Press, 1981.

677   DePauw, Linda Grant. *Seafaring Women.* Boston: Houghton Mifflin Co., 1982.

Three stories about daring women who went to sea. Includes a good bibliography.

678   English, Betty Lou. *Women at Their Work.* New York: Dial Press, 1977.

Every time the reader turns a page in this book, there is a photo of a woman in her work environment juxtaposed with a few paragraphs of her own description of how she chose a nontraditional career and what it is like. The work lives of twenty-one women are discussed. The book includes a jockey, rabbi, judge, and carpenter.

679   Epstein, Vivian Sheldon. *The History of Women for Children.* Denver: Quality Press, 1984.

Beginning with the perceived magic powers of women among cave and forest peoples and ending with the Civil Rights Act of 1964, Epstein traces how men gained power by taking it away from women. She explains gently to children that women, over the last 150 years, have set about getting that power back. She mentions what happened to women's employment during the Second World War, and she shows, through her own illustrations, some of the nontraditional work women now do. She includes women astronauts, judges, orchestral conductors, dentists, public officials, telephone repairpersons, fire fighters, mechanics, and police officers.

680   *Fortune Telling: A Program for Girls about Women, Work, and Nontraditional Occupations.* Boston: Young Women's Christian Association, 1977.

681   Gersoni-Edelman, Diane. *Work Wise: Learning about the World of Work from Books — A Critical Guide to Book Selection and Usage.* Santa Barbara, Calif.: Clio Press, 1980.

     Part 1 is about career hunting and the world of work; part 2 concerns careers, field by field.

682   Goldsmith, Judy. "Rapunzel's Revenge: Fairy Tales for Feminists." *Aurora* 10, no. 1 (Winter 1986-87): 16.

683   Hoyt, Mary Finch. *American Women of the Space Age.* New York: Atheneum, 1966.

     A young person's book introducing the many roles women have been involved in during the last twenty-five years of the U.S. space program.

684   McHugh, Mary. *The Woman Thing.* New York: Praeger Children's Books, 1973.

     The author points out occupations once considered exclusively masculine: clowns, firefighters, machinists, jockeys, truck drivers, state troopers, movie directors, pilots, umpires, and investigators for the Securities and Exchange Commission. She also discusses fields becoming more tolerant: engineering, medicine, law, architecture, business, and photography. She explains that "women's liberation seeks to free creativity in and of us by helping to avoid stereotyped thinking about one's roles in life."

685   Mitchell, Joyce Slayton. *My Mommy Makes Money.* Boston: Little Brown, 1984.

     With illustrations by True Kelley, Mitchell presents many ways mothers earn money including selling cars, playing the French horn in a symphony orchestra, repairing electrical appliances, and performing surgical operations. Written for children ages 4-7.

686   Newman, Joan E. *Girls Are People Too! A Bibliography of Nontraditional Female Roles in Children's Books.* Metuchen, N.J.: Scarecrow Press, 1982.

A guide to books about women in confident and adventurous roles, many involving work.

687   Sadker, Myra. *A Student Guide to Title IX.* Prepared for the U.S. Department of Health, Education, and Welfare, Office of Education, Resource Center on Sex Roles in Education, National Foundation for the Improvement of Education. Washington, D.C.: U.S. Government Printing Office, 45 pp.

This booklet informs students of their right to a nonsexist education and their rights and responsibilities under Title IX of the Education Amendment of 1972. Discusses schooling as a sexist activity, hidden curricula, athletics blocks, and other useful subjects.

688   Sanders, Jo Shuchat, and Stone, Antonia. *The Neuter Computer: Computers for Girls and Boys.* Prepared for the Women's Action Alliance. New York: Neal Schuman Publishers, 1986.

The book was written for everyone who wants to increase or improve computer use by children, especially girls, including: educators in high school, junior high, middle school, and elementary school; parents; students; teacher trainers in college and university education departments and in service training; and educational policy makers.

689   Siegel, Mary Ellen. *Her Way: A Guide to Biographies of Women for Young People.* Chicago: American Library Association, 1984.

Further Reading on Women in the Workplace

To understand the complexities of women at work in male-intensive fields, one needs to have a context. The context is the larger world of the American workplace itself, which is a highly complicated mirror of society. The books and articles in this section represent a few works that give insight into the meaning of work in women's lives. Many of the sources listed provide a feminist perspective on the interdisciplinary issues of workplace analysis.

690   Almquist, Elizabeth M. "Women in the Labor Force." *Signs* 2, no. 4 (Summer 1977): 843-55.
      Almquist looks at three years of sociological studies, documenting recent research on the status of women in the labor force. She finds that the research is devoid of theory, lacks policy implications, and does not predict rapid improvement in women's status in the near future. In this important article she discusses changing patterns of labor-force participation, status attainment, pay, and far-reaching suggestions for future research.

691   Amsden, Alice H., ed. *Economics of Women and Work.* New York: St. Martin's Press, 1980.
      Eighteen articles published in a variety of journals between 1962 and 1978, in three sections: "Market Work, Homework, and the Family"; "Job Segregation by Sex and Women's Lower Pay"; "Women's Employment and the Economy." In one volume, familiarizes reader with the four major critical approaches to the economics of women and work: neoclassical, institutional, Marxist, and radical.

692   Berch, Bettina. *The Endless Day: The Political Economy of Women and Work.* New York: Harcourt Brace Jovanovich, 1982.
      An undiscovered classic of feminist pedagogy. Readable summary of current research on women and work.

693   Bianchi, Suzanne. M. *Household Composition and Racial Inequality.* New Brunswick, N.J.: Rutgers University Press, 1981.

694   Bianchi, Suzanne M., and Rytina, Nancy. "The Decline in Occupational Sex Segregation during the 1970s." *Demography* 23 (February 1986): 79-86.

695　Bickner, Mei Liang. *Women at Work: An Annotated Bibliography.* Los Angeles: University of California, L.A. Institute of Industrial Relations, 1974.

696　Bickner, Mei Liang, and Shaughnessy, Marlene. *Women at Work.* Vol. 2, *An Annotated Bibliography, 1973-75.* Los Angeles: University of California, L.A. Institute of Industrial Relations, 1977.

697　Blaxall, Martha, and Reagan, Barbara, eds. *Women and the Workplace: The Implications of Occupational Segregation.* Chicago: University of Chicago Press, 1976.
　　　See entry 619 for annotation.

698　Bottini, Maria, Chertos, Cynthia, and Haignere, Lois. *Initiating Pay Equity: A Guide for Assessing Your Workplace.* Albany: State University of New York, Center for Women in Government, 1987.

699　Brodkin, Karen Sacks, and Remy, Dorothy. *My Troubles Are Going to Have Trouble with Me: Everyday Trials and Triumphs of Women Workers.* New Brunswick, N.J.: Rutgers University Press, 1984.
　　　Scholarly essays about working women in diverse settings. Title borrowed from a book by Dr. Suess in which the central character is empowered and refuses to accept setbacks.

700　Dex, Shirley. *The Sexual Division of Work: Conceptual Revolutions in the Social Sciences.* New York: St. Martin's Press, 1985.
　　　Challenging discussion of important scholarship and issues.

701　Faver, Catherine. *Women in Transition: Career, Family, and Life Satisfaction in Three Cohorts.* Westport, Conn.: Greenwood Press, 1984.

702   Ferber, Marianne A. "Women and Work: Issues of the 1980s." *Signs* 8, no. 2 (Winter 1982): 273-95.

An analysis of recent research on women's economic roles in the family and in the labor market with emphasis on the interaction between these two aspects of women's work. (See entry 620 for additional annotation.)

703   Gold, Michael Evan. *A Dialogue on Comparable Worth.* Ithaca, N.Y.: Industrial and Labor Relations Press, 1983.

Written as a debate; carefully footnoted throughout.

704   Groveman, Carol, and Norton, Mary Beth. *To Toil the Livelong Day: America's Women at Work, 1780-1980.* Ithaca, N.Y.: Cornell University Press, 1987.

Selected papers from Sixth Berkshire Conference on the History of Women, 1-3 June 1984. Mary McFeely acknowledged at beginning.

705   Gupta, Nina, comp., et al. *Exploratory Investigations of Pay for Knowledge System.* Washington, D.C.: U.S. Department of Labor, Bureau of Labor-Management Relations and Cooperative Programs, 1986.

706   Horner, Matina S. "Femininity and Successful Achievement: A Basic Inconsistency." In *Feminine Personality and Conflict,* edited by Bardwick, Judith M., et al. Belmont, Calif.: Brooks-Cole, 1970.

An important discussion of the sexist idea that if a woman is a successful achiever, she is unsuccessful at being a woman.

707   Iglehart, A. P. *Married Women and Work: 1957-1976.* Lexington, Mass.: D. C. Heath, Lexington Books, 1979.

708   Johnson, Laura Climenko, and Johnson, Robert E. *The Seam Allowance: Industrial Homework in Canada.* Toronto: Women's Press, 1982.

709 Kahn-Hut, Rachel, et al. *Women and Work: Problems and Perspectives.* New York: Oxford University Press, 1982.

   Seventeen articles published in the scholarly journal *Social Problems,* 1975-81. Could be seen as dated. Sections include: "Women and the Division of Labor"; "Limiting Assumptions"; "Home Work and Market Work"; "Systematic Segregation"; "Invisible Work: Unacknowledged Contributions"; "Women and the Dual Economy: Continuing Discrimination."

710 Kanter, Rosabeth Moss, and Stein, Barry, eds. *Life in Organizations: Workplaces As People Experience Them.* New York: Basic Books, 1979.

   The book is dedicated as follows: "For all of us who live a significant part of our lives in organizations."

711 Kessler-Harris, Alice. *Out to Work: A History of Wage-Earning Women in the U.S.* New York: Oxford University Press, 1982.

   Kessler-Harris discusses the "stranglehold of the sex-segregated workplace," among many other topics in this history of wage-earning women in the United States.

712 Kessler-Harris, Alice. *Women Have Always Worked.* Old Westbury, N.Y.: Feminist Press, 1981.

   An excellent introduction to the history of women at work.

713 Koziara, Karen Shallcross, et al. *Working Women: Past, Present, Future.* Industrial Relations Research Association Series. Washington, D.C.: Bureau of National Affairs, Industrial Relations Research Association, 1987.

   Introduction contains a summary of research knowledge and research needs. Each chapter discusses an issue and its literature. Important chapter on the minority women in the workplace (pp. 265-98).

714 Lloyd, Cynthia B., ed. *Women in the Labor Market.* New York: Columbia University Press, 1979.

715   Lloyd, Cynthia B., and Niemi, Beth T. *The Economics of Sex Differentials.* New York: Columbia University Press, 1979.

716   Lopata, Helena Z., et al. *City Women: Work, Jobs, Occupations, Careers.* 2 vols. New York: Praeger, 1984.
         This book does not get a great review from Loeb et al. (See entry 18.) Up-to-date review of literature on ten occupational groups included, however: service, blue-collar, clerical, sales, homemakers, managers, administrators, officials, professional and technical workers.

717   Matthai, Julie A. *An Economic History of Women in America: Women's Work, Sexual Division of Labor, and the Development of Capitalism.* New York: Schocken Books, 1982.
         Compare to Alice Kessler-Harris's *Out to Work* (see entry 711).

718   Medsgar, Betty. *Women at Work: A Photographic Documentary.* New York: Sheed & Ward, 1975.
         Book begins with lengthy essay by the author/photographer, then goes directly into photos and quotations. A jockey, a surgeon, a pilot, and many others are here in their work environment. Important book.

719   Meehan, Elizabeth M. *Women's Rights at Work: Campaigns and Policy in Britain and the United States.* New York: St. Martin's Press, 1985.
         Comparative historical account of equal-employment practices and policies in the United States and Britain.

720   Mott, Frank L. *The Employment Revolution: Young American Women in the 1970s.* Cambridge, Mass.: MIT Press, 1982.
         Discusses traditional versus nontraditional employment.

721   Nieva, Veronica F., and Gutek, Barbara A. *Women and Work: A Psychological Perspective.* New York: Praeger, 1981.

Literature review through 1979, excellent in quality. (See entry 102 for full annotation.)

722   Novarra, Virginia. *Women's Work, Men's Work: The Ambivalence of Equality.* New York: M. Boyars Publishers, 1980.

723   Peterson, Esther. "Working Women." *Daedalus* 93, no. 2 (Spring 1964): 671-99.
Part of special issue entitled "The Woman in America." Overview discussion with significant statistics and strong bibliography by the director of the Women's Bureau. Important statistics on attainments of black women at the time are included in this article.

724   President's Commission on the Status of Women. *American Women.* Washington, D.C.: U.S. Government Printing Office, 1963.
Presented to President Kennedy on October 11, 1963, Eleanor Roosevelt's birthday. Chaired by Eleanor Roosevelt. Esther Peterson, director of the Women's Bureau, was also on the commission. (She was also Assistant Secretary of Labor.) President Kennedy charged them "to develop plans for advancing the full partnership of men and women in our national life." This is the final report of the first American Commission on Women. Inviting the nation to encourage women to make their full contribution as citizens, the report makes strong recommendations on actions needed, education and counseling, home and community, employment, labor standards, discrimination and disadvantage, security of basic income, legal issues, and women's citizenship. It is interesting to assess the nation's progress toward achieving the goals set out in this report more than twenty-five years ago.

725   Reskin, Barbara F., and Hartmann, Heidi, eds. *Women's Work, Men's Work: Sex Segregation on the Job.* Washington, D.C.: National Academy Press, 1986.
Through the initiative of the National Research Council, the fourteen-member Committee on Women's Employment and Related Social Issues was created. Believing women's employment was in serious need of study, the committee commissioned a number of

papers, both literature reviews and original research, that were presented in 1982 at a workshop on job segregation.

This report is a product of those collective labors. It gives chilling evidence that "employment segregation by sex has grave consequences for women, men, families, and society."

Includes an excellent bibliography in addition to the provocative text.

726   Roby, Pamela. *Women in the Workplace: Proposals for Research and Policy Concerning the Conditions of Women in Industrial and Service Jobs.* Cambridge, Mass.: Schenkman Publishers, 1981.

Brief survey of literature 1890-1970. For full annotation, see entry 107.

727   Roos, Patricia. *Gender and Work: A Comparative Analysis of Industrial Societies.* Albany: State University of New York Press, 1985.

Finds the U.S. pattern of occupational sex segregation replicated throughout her sample, and demonstrates that marital status does not account for sex differences in occupational attainment.

728   Shaw, Lois Banfill, ed. *Unplanned Careers: The Working Lives of Middle-Aged Women.* Lexington, Mass.: Lexington Books, 1983.

Based on longitudinal data derived from a survey of nearly 4,000 black and white women in the United States.

729   Smith, Ralph E., ed. *The Subtle Revolution: Women at Work.* Washington, D.C.: Urban Institute Press, 1979.

730   Stromberg, Ann H., and Harkness, Shirley, eds. *Women Working: Theories and Facts in Perspective.* Palo Alto, Calif.: Mayfield, 1978.

731   Taeuber, Cynthia M., and Valdisera, Victor. *Women in the American Economy*. U.S. Bureau of the Census, Current Population Reports, ser. P-23, no. 146. Washington, D.C.: U.S. Government Printing Office, 1986.

       An analysis of the nation's population statistics regarding women at work. Many useful tables detailing changes in participation of women between 1970 and 1980 in nontraditional or male-dominated fields.

732   Tilly, Louise A., and Scott, Joan W. *Women, Work, and Family*. New York: Holt Rinehart & Winston, 1978.

733   Trieman, Donald J., and Hartmann, Heidi, eds. *Women, Work, and Wages: Equal Pay for Jobs of Equal Value*. Washington, D.C.: National Academy Press, 1981.

734   Walsh, Doris L. "What Women Want." *American Demography* 8 (June 1986): 60.

       This article analyzes the latest findings in the Roper Organization's national opinion poll conducted for Virginia Slims. According to Walsh, the poll is an important benchmark because it has asked a nationally representative sample of men and women the same questions for fifteen years. It reflects significant shifts in attitude and life-styles over fifteen years, and this time it shows that as women have gained more confidence and independence, a significant proportion of men have adapted well.

735   Wallace, Phyllis A., ed. *Women in the Workplace*. Boston: Auburn House, 1982.

       Papers contributed by Lotte Bailyn, Anne Harlan, Brigid O'Farrell, and Phyllis Wallace, among others. Contains an appendix with the full text of the "Equal Employment Opportunity Commission Guidelines on Discrimination because of Sex."

736   Weiner, Lynn Y. *From Working Girl to Working Mother: The Female Labor Force in the United States, 1820-1980.* Chapel Hill: University of North Carolina Press, 1985.

737   Zalokar, N. "Generational Differences in Female Occupational Attainment." *American Economical Review* 76 (May 1986): 378-81.

Author Index

Subject Index

Title Index

The Author

Carroll Wetzel Wilkinson is the interim head of circulation services and an associate university librarian at the West Virginia University Libraries in Morgantown, West Virginia. Born in Chicago, Illinois, she holds an M.L.S. from Rutgers University in New Brunswick, New Jersey, and B.A. from Wells College in Aurora, New York.

She was the chairperson of the WVU Council for Women's Concerns in 1984-87 and the 1988 winner of the Mary Catherine Bushwell Award for outstanding service to the women of West Virginia University. She is a member of the American Library Association, the Association for College and Research Libraries, and the ACRL Women's Studies Section.